CUSTOMER & SERVICE SYSTEMS

SPECIAL ISSUE: CUSTOMER EMPOWERMENT

Volume 1 | Number 1 | May 2014

CUSTOMER & SERVICE SYSTEMS

SPECIAL ISSUE: CUSTOMER EMPOWERMENT
Volume 1 | Number 1 | May 2014

Andreas Geyer-Schulz Informationsdienste und elektronische Märkte,
Karlsruhe Institute of Technology (KIT), Karlsruhe,
E-mail: andreas.geyer-schulz@kit.edu

Lars Meyer-Waarden University Toulouse 1, CRM CNRS &
EM Strasbourg, HuManiS,
E-mail: meyerwaarden@em-strasbourg.eu

Customer & Service Systems is an interdisciplinary journal at the crossroads of marketing, management information systems, and computer science. It is a forum for high standard publications on research and applications focusing on:

• New products, technologies, their service systems and infrastructures.
• Their acceptance and value for customers.
• Their short and long-term effects on enterprises, industries, and society.

The journal encourages a broad spectrum of contributions in the field of Customer & Service Systems including conceptual, theoretical, methodological, and empirical articles.

Impressum

 Scientific Publishing

Karlsruher Institut für Technologie (KIT)
KIT Scientific Publishing
Straße am Forum 2
D-76131 Karlsruhe

KIT Scientific Publishing is a registered trademark of Karlsruhe Institute of Technology. Reprint using the book cover is not allowed.

www.ksp.kit.edu

Print on Demand 2014

ISSN 2198-8005
ISBN 978-3-7315-0178-7
DOI 10.5445/KSP/1000038784

Contents

Consumer Empowerment: What and Why?

Andreas Geyer-Schulz and Lars Meyer-Waarden

The second French-German workshop about *Consumer Empowerment* took place at the University of Karlsruhe (KIT) between January 10–11, 2013. Within the scope of consumer empowerment scientists discussed recent developments in this field and established cross-disciplinary cooperations in their own fields of research.

Consumer empowerment is deeply rooted in the human dreams and phantasies of a good life: The Jinns in *Aladdin and the Enchanted Lamp* – one of the most famous stories of *One Thousand and One Nights* translated by Antoine Galland in 1709 – empower and enable the bearer of the enchanted lamp to fulfill all his wishes and desires (Fulda, 1912). But scientists do not believe in Jinns: Today, technological progress has brought this dream to the brink of realization: Internet services as modern Jinns empower and enable consumers to participate in new ways in the design, production, and fulfillment of products and services for their wants. Pierre Teilhard de Chardin's vision of the future of man (Teilhard de Chardin, 1963) rests on the extrapolation of biological and social evolution: he predicts that the human race will evolve and will reach a transhuman stage (ultra human). With the rapid development

Andreas Geyer-Schulz
Informationsdienste und elektronische Märkte, Karlsruhe Institute of Technology (KIT), Karlsruhe
✉ andreas.geyer-schulz@kit.edu

Lars Meyer-Waarden
University Toulouse 1, CRM CNRS & EM Strasbourg, HuManiS
✉ meyerwaarden@em-strasbourg.eu

CUSTOMER & SERVICE SYSTEMS
KIT SCIENTIFIC PUBLISHING
Vol. 1, No. 1, S. 1–17, 2014

DOI 10.5445/KSP/1000038784/01
ISSN 2198-8005

of a technology-driven ubiquituous service system (the Jinns), consumer empowerment adds technological progress as a new dimension to man's evolution: Even today, service systems give man ultra human capabilities.

Consumer power and empowerment are multi-faceted phenomena. Consumer empowerment is a firm-initiated strategy to increase consumers' control over their marketing process (co-design, recommendation). This firm-controlled transfer of power results in positive outcomes of consumer collaborations in the form of the firms' co-designed offer. However, consumer empowerment also might lead to undesired or uncontrolled transfers of power, such that it entails a rejection of intrusion (advertisements, market research) or individual (negative word-of-mouth) or collective actions (boycotts). Yet, these multiple faces are not clearly defined. Furthermore, despite the centrality of consumer power for marketing practice we still struggle to understand the forces behind these phenomena, both theoretically and empirically. A recent survey of these struggles is e.g. Denegri-Knott et al (2006).

To start and to understand this paradigm shift we have to look closer to the history and evolution of marketing and management. Originally the autonomous, self-determined, sovereign and empowered consumactor was the anti-consumer – a citizen engaged in fair trade, whose purchase was a citizen act. This led to collective consumerist movements, such as collective boycotts of goods from a company whose business practices are deemed unfair (Friedman, 1996). But this consumactor gently drifted towards a less ethically engaged individual and became a smartshopper in times of crisis (Bearden et al, 1984; Blattberg et al, 1978; Schindler, 1998). These creative agents adopt tactics to counteract the strategic maneuvers of firms, they are not powerless dupes manipulated by marketers (Abercrombie, 1994). The last evolution is that this consumactor expects the brands to offer opportunities to become an "artist" of marketing and design. Today, the consumer claims the role of a creator. Based on this, companies have built marketing strategies which are centered on the power transfer to consumers.

Historically, marketing came to this point, because the centralized, unilateral version of mass marketing and management, as practiced for more than 50 years, had achieved its limits, such that it no longer creates value for either customers or the firm. With the rise of information technologies, a customer who previously seemed recognizable and stereotypical might today disappear into multiple identities on the Internet which existing marketing logics could not track. Customer relationship management (CRM) and mass customization thus have become crucial (Franke et al, 2009, 2010), but as is common for many innovations, most firms have been guided simply by imitation rather than by a real initiative to differentiate themselves from their competition. CRM thus has marked a beginning of this trend, but has often perverted individualization for purposes of productivity using mass customization and automation too much. The euphoria of marketing academics and managers (e.g. Malone, 1998) thus has given way to disillusionment, along with consumer resistance and decreasing marketing performance indicators, including loyalty and satisfaction (Meyer-Waarden, 2012).

In the meantime, a new marketing paradigm has emerged to empower consumers (Prahalad and Ramaswamy, 2000; Fuchs et al, 2010) through a shift of market power from suppliers to consumers, in connection with the increasing use of information technologies (Malone, 1997). Consumer empowerment is rooted in a background trend: the return to the individual consumer. Marketers have to start from him/her and have to return to him/her – a fact that had been completely neglected for decades by traditional mass marketing.

Consumer empowerment as firm-initiated and controlled transfer of power results in positive outcomes of consumer collaborations in the form of the firms' co-designed offer with the goal of delivering a higher value at less costs to more customers (Von Hippel et al, 1999; Prahalad and Ramaswamy, 2000; Franke et al, 2009, 2010). Co-production, the lowest stage of empowerment, is an old example where companies seek to appropriate the consumer's abilities with the only target to reduce costs. IKEA and McDonalds have built their strategies on this principle successfully. Co-creation is the highest level of consumer empowerment. Innovation and product/service creation, traditionally considered the domain of R&D, are there outsourced to consumers. The new challenge, therefore, is giving the consumer the right tools and services to collaborate and – to motivate them to co-create or co-produce value. This change leads to the transformation of CRM from a generator of knowledge about the customer into CRM as the creator of knowledge together with the customer. There are thus a lot of positive outcomes of consumer empowerment. The co-creation of value for the customer might result in value for the company through increased willingness to pay and increased loyalty (Kumar et al, 2006). Consumer empowerment modifies the notion of value, because the consumer determines the value of a product by producing or using it and not through the manufacturer's production efforts. The consumer also must learn to use and maintain the product, as well as adapt it to his unique needs, situations, or behaviors. This assertion constitutes the point of departure in the evolution of marketing towards a service dominant logic (Vargo and Lusch, 2004).

Yet this transfer of power may not be desired or controlled well by firms, especially if consumers are conscious of their power, competencies, and expertise. In this case, consumers may manipulate marketer-intended meanings, engage in negative word of mouth (WOM; Villanueva et al, 2008) or refuse to co-produce or co-create (Franke et al, 2009, 2010). According to Forrester Research (2010), U.S. consumers generate 500 billion WOM impressions of products every year (Bernoff et al, 2010), and they are perceived as more credible than marketing messages. The transfer of power also could lead to destruction, rejection (e.g. consumerist movements, boycotts, avoidance), and, last but not least, resistance to consumption. In summary, marketing implications arising from consumer empowerment can be examined in terms of a process that makes control and management by firms over consumer access increasingly difficult. A rich tradition of criticizing marketing practice as a powerful economic, social institution designed to control and dominate consumers still exists though. Despite the important consequences of such responses, especially in new forms of public spaces (e.g. Internet, collaborative platforms), academic research on consumer empowerment remains scarce in the management science literature.

Due to technology and digital media based service systems – the modern Jinns – this transfer of power has taken place. Without mobile web and web 2.0 this development – the transfer of power to the consumer – would not have happened. More than three decades ago the economic role of these modern Jinns and their impact on competition has been discussed in computer science by Black Ives and Gerard P. Learmonth in their 1984 landmark paper *The Information System as a Competitive Weapon* (Ives and Learmonth, 1984) from an information systems development point of view. The authors describe tactical changes in the information systems of companies which support the strategic aspect of customer/consumer empowerment by enabling customers/consumers to participate in business processes in a different way. The rise of digital media more than any other media finally allowed this recovery of the relationship in its original sense by the consideration to transfer power to the individual. Digital media transform the brand into a person with which the consumer can initiate a conversation, to develop a real relationship (which was the initial idea and real essence of relationship marketing when the concept appeared first in the academic service marketing research in the 1980ies (Berry, 1983, 1995; Groenroos, 1984; Morgan and Hunt, 1994). Digital media provide simple, helpful and hedonistic empowerment tools. Crowdsourcing is one of them. There are many other tools. It is interesting to note that empowerment carries two distinct and complementary aspects. The original meaning of empowerment (operate the suggestions of consumers) has been enriched by another dimension, co-creation which is the nirvana of the empowerment process, because the client becomes actor of innovation and the products'/services' creation process in the firm.

The fine-grained customer/consumer resource life cycle (CRLC) describes the generic model of an integrated business process between customer/consumer and supplier which covers the whole product/service lifecycle: The concept is illustrated by a host of practical examples of IT-enabled changes in process steps and their early adopters. Reread from todays' perspective, we see that all the changes suggested have become reality, but that the early innovators have not become the new global players.

In the invited lecture *Collaborative Consumption: Does Materialism Contribute to Sharing?* Christophe Benavent, professor at the university Paris Nanterre, investigated the propensity of the consumer to share products or services with other consumers depending on the product or service category. His motivating example Airbnb (www.airbnb.com) – the leading internet platform for sharing rooms between consumers – is an example of a service which supports the process step *Select a Source* in the CRLC model.

Benavent's lecture on Airbnb led to a spirited discussion on the nature of transformative services and it raised the problem of a strategic reorganization of industries and how to analyze the strategic options.

Transformative service research has a very broad research agenda (including the planning, building, and managing of service infrastructures) that relates to and advocates the personal and collective well-being of consumers and societies (Rosenbaum et al, 2011). A transformative ser-

vice is defined as "a service or a product that centers on creating up-
lifting changes and improvements in the well-being of both individuals
and communities" (Ostrom et al, 2010). This research identifies issues
related to supporting and enhancing well-being outcomes, which may include among other things, consumer experiences, consumers' freedom,
control and agency, as well as their social networks and services, their
happiness, and a mitigation of their vulnerability as consumers.

In the case of Airbnb, the availability of a global intermediation service on a provision base has started to change the tourism industry and
also the rental market for apartments in attractive areas. The structural
industry changes made possible by Airbnb basically empower and enable
consumers to provide almost all accomodation related services of a hotel
to other consumers (Amann and Tietz, 2013). However, in addition the
change also has disruptive social effects: The availability of affordable
housing for the working class is considerably reduced and the quality
of living for regular inhabitants is negatively affected. In Berlin, about
600 000 guest beds are already offered on such platforms: A black room
market is on the rise (Niedermeier, 2012).

In his book *Niche Envy: Marketing Discrimination in the Digital Age*
(Turow, 2006), Joseph Turow analyzes the global advertising industry –
another industry undergoing drastic technological change – from a marketing perspective. His analysis shows that marketing communication
and its instruments (e.g. product placements, direct selling, guerilla marketing, viral marketing, in-store displays, email, sampling, e-commerce,
...) have become dominant. The changes are technologically driven: Customer information gained from customer profiling leads to customized
advertising, content, and pricing. Information technology shows its Janus
faces: There is an inevitable trade-off between customer/consumer conve-
nience and well-being and privacy. Trust-building and trust destroying
activities hang in a delicate balance.

The analysis of potential changes in industry structures has been a
major concern in the development of e-commerce: Schlueter and Shaw
(1997) and, applied to the integration patterns in electronic channels,
Schlueter-Langdon and Shaw (2002) provide a two-layer/ three-stage
framework for the analysis of value chains and value-adding activities
of the digital interactive service (DIS) industries. The framework is built
from a generic 2-3-6 industry structure (2 layers, 3 stages, 6 sets of core
activities) by defining strategic roles on top of the industry structure

for certain scenarios. Christoph Schlueter-Langdon and Michael Shaw have investigated potential structural changes for the following industries: publishing, retailing, financial and travel services. Almost all of the analyzed changes support customer/consumer empowerment and enablement – albeit with a deficit on the marketing side.

Now, let us return to the tale of *Aladdin and the Enchanted Lamp*. We consider the tale as a metaphor for a modern service system: From a system analysis point of view, the Jinns and the Enchanted Lamp form the visible part of the service system, and the service production system the Jinns use is invisible. Rubbing the lamp and ordering the Jinns is an easy to use end-user interface comparable to Apple's iPhone interface.

Marketers concentrate their research on the visible part: the customers/consumers and their wishes and the various ways of interaction with the service system. The service system itself is considered as a black box. Management information systems specialists and computer scientists, on the other hand, see the service system as a white box and they emphasize the design and the analysis of the interior of the white box according to system requirements specifications.

Communication across the system boundary is severely hampered. We illustrate this communication breakdown and lack of interdisciplinarity by two examples which show the importance of an easy-to use, reliable, and faultless service system for customer/consumer empowerment:

1. Marketers discovered that out-of-stock situations and delivery problems were a main problem of early e-commerce sites empowering the consumer for home-shopping (e.g. Holloway and Beatty, 2003). However, a root cause analysis is missing in these papers. For a management information system specialist, a glance on the architecture of web-shops reveals that customer/consumer interactions were not properly encapsulated as transactions with ACID-properties (Atomicity, Consistency, Isolation, Durability) over several system components. This type of architecture is still thought to be acceptable in many organizations because of the cost advantages of building only loosely coupled systems without end-to-end transaction concepts and the assumption of system analysts that race conditions are unlikely to occur.

2. The problem of measuring technology acceptance of end-users is an active area of research in computer science, management information

systems research and, last but not least, in marketing. However, the analysis of recent articles in top journals of the three fields (Seiffer, 2013) show three independent clusters of research:

a. Computer scientists (and the computer industry) rely and use the 4 part ISO/IEC Software Engineering - Product Quality Standard from 2001–2004 (see, ISO/IEC, 2001, 2003a,b, 2004). Especially, the fourth part of the product quality standard (ISO/IEC 9126-4) on quality in use metrics is relevant for technology acceptance and thus customer empowerment. The product quality standard is derived from work of the human computer interface (HCI) community from 1980 to 1995 and, especially of IBM. For references, see (ISO/IEC, 2004, p. 46).

b. In management information systems, most published investigations use the technology acceptance model (TAM). See Davis (1985, 1989) or one of its variants (Venkatesh and Davis, 2000). Recent surveys of the TAM model are given by Chuttur (2009) and Turner et al (2010). As these two reviews show, the link between technology acceptance, actual use of a technology and thus customer empowerment is receiving considerable attention in the management information systems community.

c. In marketing, researchers have proposed a host of different models with different operationalizations of the same latent constructs. As examples of this line of research, we refer to Parasuraman's Technology Readiness Index (Parasuraman, 2000) and the work of Dabholkar (1991, 1996), and Reinders et al (2008) on the evaluations of consumer self-service options.

Cross-references and an analysis of the overlap and differences between the research work in the three disciplines are missing completely. In the age of the wide (global) availability and electronic dissemination of scientific publications this is both surprising and shocking.

Empowerment, participative and collaborative consumption, co-construction, co-production, co-creation are common denominators of a consumer orientated phenomenon. Regardless of the name, these trends will merge into only one single strategy. Marketers will have to think without borders. They will have to establish a digital strategy. Closed silos with brand strategies, digital strategies, information system strategies, and, social networking strategies are done and obsolete. An empowered consumer requires to lift the participatory level to the brand strategy and to make digital strategy evolve into a social strategy. The challenge is important because a consumer who is not listened to nor understood, who is not engaged by the brand, who cannot not participate, will be a disinterested consumer whose chances of defection will increase. The individual must be placed into the centre as brands too often tend to forget humans and their well being.

Customer/consumer empowerment and customer/consumer enablement therefore is a fascinating new interdisciplinary research field which requires the seamless integration of research from marketing, management information systems and computer science. We, therefore, focus in our investigations on these and other related issues in order to stimulate further considerations and research.

The 16 contributions in this book (listed alpabetically by author) focus on customer empowerment and have been presented at the 2nd French-German Workshop Customer/Consumer Empowerment (KIT, Karlsruhe, 10th-11th January, 2013). They give a snapshot of the work in progress in the emerging field *customer / consumer empowerment* of a group of 29 French-German researchers in Marketing, Computer Science and Management Information Systems:

1. In the contribution *The Long-term Impact of Sales Promotions on Customer Equity* Herbert Castéran and Lars Meyer-Waarden study the long term effects of sales promotions by integrating promotion-related explanatory variables into stochastic consumer behavior models. The introduction of explanatory variables considerably improves the model quality. Finally, the positive or negative impact of promotions on customer equity depends on brands (national/private label) and promotion types (monetary/non-monetary).
2. Sihem Dekhili and Chantal Connan Guesquière discuss the very controversial issue of tranferring the power of price setting to the consumer in their contribution *The "Pay What You Want" Pricing Policy: Power Sharing or Communication Action?*.
3. Rewarding a customer with an elavated status based on repeat-purchases or spending level is a classic incentive in hierarchical loyalty programs. But what happens if firms offer customers an elevated

status who have not earned it? In their contribution *How Profound Is the Allure of Endowed Status in Hierarchical Loyalty Programs?* Andreas Eggert, Ina Garnefeld and Lena Steinhoff report on experimental evidence on the bright and the dark sides of status endowment.

4. Andreas Geyer-Schulz and Michael Ovelgönne's contribution *Recent Advances in Modularity Optimization and Their Application in Retailing* reports on the algorithmic progress in graph-clustering and its potential for customer empowerment and enablement in several types of retail applications.

5. The customer as a co-producer and his willingness to pay is investigated in a series of innovative experiments (mainly with regard to transferability and degree of co-production activities) by Nicola Bilstein, Jens Hogreve, Christina Sichtmann and René Fahr. In their contribution *Paying for a higher Workload? The Relation between Customer's Co-Production and Willingness to Pay* they present their findings.

6. Martin Klarmann and Johannes Habel investigate the link between downsizing and customer satisfaction and its moderators in their contribution *Mass Layoffs: When and How Do They Affect Customer Satisfaction?*. They combine data from the American Customer Satisfaction Index with data from Compustat and survey data.

7. The contribution *Complaint Management and the Role of Relationship Quality* by Lars Meyer-Waarden and William Sabadie reports on the respondents' reactions to a compensation activity selected from a set of 8 compensation scenarios. The authors find that the nature of compensation as well as its value and the way it is communicated strongly depend on the customer type.

8. In their contribution *Customer-to-Customer Interactions within Online Review Sites: A Typology of Contributors* Andreas Munzel and Werner H. Kunz study the motivation of consumers with regard to eWOM. Based on a survey of eWOM activities and motives, they identify three types of consumers of a hotel online review site, namely lurkers, creators, and multipliers.

9. In the paper *Converting Opinion Seekers in Opinion Givers in the Tourism Industry: Building Trust Is Critical!* Gilles N'Goala and Caroline Morrongiello investigate which antecedents are relevant for consumer participation and engagement on the Web 2.0. The main con-

tribution is that most tourists want to help their companies/resorts and that the perceived sincerity of online reviews has a large impact on participation and engagement.

10. The contribution *How Web 2.0 Tools Impact The Museum-Visitor Relationship* by Jessie Pallud explores the changes in the relationship between museums and their visitors caused and made possible by social media. The reason for this development is the need for museums to adopt a competitive strategy in order to cope with competition from other leisure and entertainment activities and with budget reductions by governments.

11. Daria Plotkina, Andreas Munzel return to the origin of the word-of-mouth effect: Customers spread their positive experiences with new products by chatting in their social environment. In their contribution *What's New With You! On the Moderating Effect of Product Novelty on eWOM Effectiveness* they propose an experimental framework based on a between-subject factorial design to study the effect of product novelty.

12. Claire Roederer and Marc Filser outline a research agenda for investigating the cyber-experience of various types Internet-based consumer interactions (including co-production and co-creation) in their article *e-Voicing an Opinion on a Brand - A Research Agenda*.

13. In the *The Contribution of Gratitude to Satisfaction Models for Complaining Customers* Françoise Simon, Chantal Connan Guesquière and Vesselina Tossan investigate the effects of gratitude and transactional satisfaction on purchase intent and word-of-mouth in a complaint situation. They find that while transactional satisfaction has an impact on word-of-mouth, gratitude impacts purchase intent.

14. Andreas Sonnenbichler discusses the problems of consumer privacy, empowerment and enablement on Facebook by considering an appropriate access control model. In his contribution *Social Access Control* he analyzes the current Facebook access control model and identifies four classes of users with different requirements for access control. He introduces the Access Definition and Query Language (ADQL) and suggests this language as a tool for modeling and implementing personalized access control in Facebook.

15. Loyalty programs have boomed in recent years. However, these marketing tools almost never were profitable. The contribution *Understanding the Effectiveness of Loyalty Programs* by Lena Steinhoff and

Robert W. Palmatier provides a new framework that links gratitude, status, and fairness with customer loyalty and profitability. Their framework separates the measurement of direct effects on customers receiving loyalty program rewards from the measurement of indirect effects on customers not receiving rewards.

16. In their contribution *Lead-users vs. Emergent Nature Consumers for Marketing Co-creation: Are They Really Different?* Eric Vernette and Linda Hamdi-Kidar assess the similarity and differences of the latent constructs `lead-user` and `emergent nature consumer`. They conduct a web-based questionnaire survey of French video-game players and their main finding is that a refinement of the concept of `lead-user` into a `global lead-user` and a `specific lead-user` is possible and that the concept of a `global lead-user` is highly related with the concept of a emergent nature consumer in the sense that both concepts share similar traits.

We hope that you will enjoy these first insights of our research about consumer empowerment. Other workshops about the topic will follow and will be published. The next workshop will be co-organised on May 13th and 14th, 2014 by EM-Strasbourg Business School (Humanis) and the Institute of Informationsdienste und elektronische Märkte – KIT at the University of Montpellier. Finally, the editors of this book are very indebted to all colleagues who participated and/or reviewed papers for this volume. We gratefully acknowledge the help and support as well as the active cooperation of all participants and authors. We would like to emphasize the excellent work of all assistants and secretaries involved in the organization of the conference and preparation of this proceedings volume. Especially, we thank Mrs. Victoria-Anne Schweigert for organizing the workshop and its social program and Mr. Maximilian Korndörfer for his support in typesetting and LaTeX conversion.

We hope that the presented volume will find interested readers and that it encourages further research about emerging consumer behaviors and company strategies such as empowerment.

Karlsruhe, Strasbourg and Toulouse, August 2013
Andreas Geyer-Schulz and Lars Meyer-Waarden

References

Abercrombie N (1994) Authority and consumer society. In: Keat et al (1994), chap 2, pp 43 – 57

Amann S, Tietz J (2013) Teile und herrsche. Der Spiegel 2013(2):60 – 62

Bearden WO, Lichtenstein DR, Teel JE (1984) Comparison price, coupon, and brand effects on consumer reactions to retail newspaper advertisements. Journal of Retailing 60(2):11 – 34

Bernoff J, Ray A, Wise J (2010) Peer influence analysis – a social computing report. mass influencers are the key to achieving scale in social media marketing. Tech. Rep. E-RES56766, Forrester Research

Berry L (1995) Relationship marketing of services–growing interest, emerging perspectives. Journal of the Academy of Marketing Science 23(4):236 – 245

Berry LL (1983) Relationship marketing. In: Berry et al (1983), pp 25 – 28

Berry LL, Shostack G, Upah G (eds) (1983) Emerging Perspectives on Services Marketing. American Marketing Association, Chicago

Blattberg R, Buesing T, Peacock P, Sen S (1978) Identifying the deal prone segment. Journal of Marketing Research (JMR) 15(3):369 – 377

Bradley S, Nolan RL (eds) (1998) Sense & Respond: Capturing Value in the Network Era. Harvard Business School Press, Boston

Teilhard de Chardin P (1963) Die Zukunft des Menschen, Werke Theilhard de Chardins, vol 5. Walter-Verlag, Olten

Chuttur M (2009) Overview of the technology acceptance model: Origins, developments and future directions. Sprouts: Working Papers on Information Systems 9(37):1 – 21

Dabholkar PA (1991) Decision making in consumer trial of technology-based self-service options: An attitude-based choice model. PhD thesis, Georgia State University

Dabholkar PA (1996) Consumer evaluations of new technology-based self-service options: An investigation of alternative models of service quality. International Journal of Research in Marketing 13 (1):29 – 51

Davis F (1985) A technology acceptance model for empirically testing new end-user information systems: Theory and results. PhD thesis, Massachusetts Institute of Technology

Davis F (1989) Perceived usefulness, perceived ease of use, and user acceptance of information technology. MIS Quarterly 13(3):319 – 340

Denegri-Knott J, Zwick D, Schroeder JE (2006) Mapping consumer power: An integrative framework for marketing and consumer research. European Journal of Marketing 40(9/10):950 – 971

Franke N, Keinz P, Steger CJ (2009) Testing the value of customization: When do customers really prefer products tailored to their preferences? Journal of Marketing 73(9):103 – 121

Franke N, Schreier M, Kaiser U (2010) The "I designed it myself" effect in mass customization. Management Science 56(1):125 – 140

Friedman M (1996) A positive approach to organized consumer action: The "buycott" as an alternative to the boycott. Journal of Consumer Policy 19(4):439 – 451

Fuchs C, Prandelli E, Schreier M (2010) The psychological effects of empowerment strategies on consumers' product demand. Journal of Marketing 74(1):65 – 79

Fulda L (1912) Aladdin und die Wunderlampe. Unbekannt. Projekt Gutenberg (2004)., Berlin

Groenroos C (1984) A service quality model and its marketing implications. European Journal of Marketing 18(4):36 – 44

Holloway BB, Beatty SE (2003) Service failure in online retailing: A recovery opportunity. Journal of Service Research 6(1):92 – 105

ISO/IEC (2001) Software engineering – product quality – part 1: Quality model. Tech. Rep. ISO/IEC-9126-1, International Standardization Organisation/International Electrotechnical Commission

ISO/IEC (2003a) Software engineering – product quality – part 2: External metrics. Tech. Rep. ISO/IEC-9126-2, International Standardization Organisation/International Electrotechnical Commission

ISO/IEC (2003b) Software engineering – product quality – part 3: Internal metrics. Tech. Rep. ISO/IEC-9126-3, International Standardization Organisation/International Electrotechnical Commission

ISO/IEC (2004) Software engineering – product quality – part 4: Quality in use metrics. Tech. Rep. ISO/IEC-9126-4, International Standardization Organisation/International Electrotechnical Commission

Ives B, Learmonth GP (1984) The information system as a competitive weapon. Communications of the ACM 27(12):1193 – 1201

Keat R, Abercrombie N, Whitley N (eds) (1994) The Authority of the Consumer. Routledge, London

Kumar V, Lemon KN, Parasuraman A (2006) Managing customers for value: An overview and research agenda. Journal of Service Research 9(2):87 – 94

Malone TW (1997) Is empowerment just a fad? Control, decision making, and IT. Sloan Management Review 38(2):23 – 35

Malone TW (1998) Inventing the organizations of the twenty-first century: Control, empowerment, and information technology. In: Bradley and Nolan (1998), chap 12, pp 263 – 285

Meyer-Waarden L (2012) Management de la fidélisation – Développer la relation client: de la stratétegie aux technologies numériques. Eds. Vuibert, Paris

Morgan RM, Hunt SD (1994) The commitment-trust theory of relationship marketing. Journal of Marketing 58(3):20

Niedermeier R (2012) Ärger mit den neuen Nachbarn: Privatwohnung statt Hotel – Social Travel ist oft alles andere als sozial. Badische Neuste Nachrichten (BNN) 2012(42)

Ostrom AL, Bitner MJ, Brown SW, Burkhard KA, Goul M, Smith-Daniels V, Demirkan H, Rabinovich E (2010) Moving forward and making a difference: Research priorities for the science of service. Journal of Service Research 13(1):4 – 36

Parasuraman A (2000) Technology readiness index (TRI): A multiple-item scale to measure readiness to embrace new technologies. Journal of Service Research 2(4):307 – 320

Prahalad CK, Ramaswamy V (2000) Co-opting customer competence. Harvard Business Review 78(1):79 – 87

Reinders MJ, Dabholkar PA, Frambach RT (2008) Consequences of forcing consumers to use technology-based self-service. Journal of Service Research 11(2):107 – 123

Rosenbaum MS, Corus C, Ostrom AL, Anderson L, Fisk RP, Gallan AS, Giraldo M, Mende M, Mulder M (2011) Conceptualization and aspirations of transformative service research. Journal of Research for Consumers 19:1 – 6

Schindler RM (1998) Consequences of perceiving oneself as responsible for obtaining a discount: Evidence for smart-shopper feelings. Journal of Consumer Psychology (Lawrence Erlbaum Associates) 7(4):371

Schlueter C, Shaw MJ (1997) A strategic framework for developing electronic commerce. IEEE Internet Computing 1(6):20 – 28

Schlueter-Langdon C, Shaw MJ (2002) Emergent patterns of integration in electronic channel systems. Communications of the ACM 45(12):50 – 55

Seiffer A (2013) Determinants of consumer's intention to use and their actual use of technology: A comparison of established models (bachelor thesis). PhD thesis, KIT, Karlsruhe, preliminary Draft.

Turner M, Kitchenham B, Brereton P, Charters S, Budgen D (2010) Does the technology acceptance model predict actual use? A systematic literature review. Information and Software Technology 52:463 – 479

Turow J (2006) Niche Envy: Marketing Discrimination in the Digital Age. MIT Press, Cambridge, Massachusetts

Vargo SL, Lusch RF (2004) Evolving to a new dominant logic for marketing. Journal of Marketing 68(1):1 – 17

Venkatesh V, Davis F (2000) A theoretical extension of the technology acceptance model: Four longitudinal field studies. Management Science 46 (2):186 – 204

Villanueva J, Yoo S, Hanssens DM (2008) The impact of marketing-induced versus word-of-mouth customer acquisition on customer equity growth. Journal of Marketing Research (JMR) 45(1):48 – 59

Von Hippel E, Thomke S, Sonnack M (1999) Creating breakthroughs at 3M. Harvard Business Review 77(5):47 – 57

The Long-Term Impact of Sales Promotions on Customer Equity

Herbert Castéran and Lars Meyer-Waarden

Abstract Sales promotion is an instrument whose effectiveness for short-term sales is proven (Blattberg and Neslin, 1990). But for the long term, researchers have identified adverse effects without managing to actually determine its impact (Van Heerde et al, 2004). While most investigations analyze the effects of promotions on sales, it is important to consider the global impact, i.e. on the customer portfolio. Although several authors have taken up this issue (Fader and Hardie, 2010; Abe, 2009b), no contribution has integrated the entire portfolio development: customer acquisition, activity of existing customers and churn.

This research, therefore, contributes by establishing a long-term vision of the impact of sales promotions on the value of the customer portfolio (customer equity), not just on sales. We combine explanatory and stochastic approaches via the integration of explanatory variables. The second contribution is the application of these models to fast moving consumer goods, a sector that has thus far been over-looked by existing research.

Herbert Castéran
EM Strasbourg Business School, HuManiS (EA 1347), 61 Avenue de la Forêt Noire, 67085 Strasbourg Cedex, France
✉ herbert.casteran@gmail.com

Lars Meyer-Waarden
University Toulouse 1, CRM CNRS & EM Strasbourg, HuManiS
✉ meyerwaarden@em-strasbourg.eu

CUSTOMER & SERVICE SYSTEMS
KIT SCIENTIFIC PUBLISHING
Vol. 1, No. 1, S. 19–24, 2014

DOI 10.5445/KSP/1000038784/02
ISSN 2198-8005

1 Conceptual Framework and Hypotheses

The customer portfolio is the central concept on which the customer relationship management strategy and the assessment of the marketing efficiency are based. The total asset value of this portfolio is the customer equity. The switch from individual customer analysis to customer portfolio analysis must result in the integration of the global risk (Gupta et al, 2006). A desirable customer, therefore, is a customer who decreases the risk and not just a customer with a strong profitability potential.

Since the 2000s, there appears to be a consensus on the long-term harmlessness of promotions but without clear results (Slotegraaf and Pauwels, 2008). Several authors essentially analyze the effects of promotions on sales in a way that makes it impossible to determine whether the promotion ultimately creates or destroys value. Therefore, the use of a global metric, customer equity, is recommended (Van Heerde et al, 2004). Our hypotheses are the following:

H1   Acquisition via monetary promotions reduces the new customer equity.
H2   Customer acquisition via non-monetary promotions increases the new customer equity.
H3   Monetary promotions reduce the global brand's customer equity.
H4   Non-monetary promotions increase the global brand's customer equity.
H5   Monetary and non-monetary promotions have a stronger impact on the global customer equity of brands with strong brand equity.

2 Methodology

The data is derived from the coffee category of the French *BehaviorScan* panel. The initial file includes 6,284 households that belong to the same cohort.

Two types of non-monetary promotion are characterized in the form of a dichotomous variable: aisle end display promotions and leaflet promotions. We consider a price reduction equal to or higher than 5% from one week to the next, until the prices go up again, as a promotion (Helsen and

Schmittlein, 1992). Our analysis is restricted to two EAN (European Article Numbering) codes: the best-selling national brand product and the best-selling private label brand product.

The Customer Equity (CE) modeling process must take into account four phenomena: a) the acquisition of a new customer, b) the customer activity and c) residual transaction, d) the average expenditures.

a) *Acquisition.* The probability of becoming a customer is given by a Cox proportional hazards model.

b) *Customer activity residual transaction.* The beta-geometric / negative binomial distribution (BG/NBD) model is the easiest and the most efficient formulation (Abe, 2009a; Fader et al, 2005b). In order to take into account explanatory variables, we follow the method advocated by Fader and Hardie (2007) as well as Castéran et al (2007).

c) *Expenditures per transaction.* The average expenditures per transaction are estimated by the gamma-gamma model (Fader et al, 2005a). We introduced explanatory variables in the gamma-gamma model.

We measure the effect of promotions via a 50% increase in the number of promotions, after which we observe the difference between the forecasts of the models associated with this increase and those of constant promotion models. The forecast period is set at 5 years. We set the discount rate at 1.5% per annum, which is similar to the opportunity costs used to evaluate investment projects.

3 Results

For customer acquisition models, the adjustment quality of these models is more than satisfactory. The BG/NBD model with explanatory variables is considerably more efficient than the one without explanatory variables. Concerning the monetary model, the Bayesian Information Criterion (BIC) improves significantly with explanatory variables. This criterion should be preferred to the Akaike Information Criterion (AIC) because it clearly reduces the risk of overfitting. It should be noted that this impact measures, in relation to a non-promotion situation, the evolutions of customer equity following a 50% increase in promotions.

H1 is validated: acquisition via monetary promotions reduces the new customer equity for national brands (-12%) or has no significant im-

Table 1 Impact of a 50% increase in monetary & non-monetary promotions

Evolutions	Price	Leaflet	Aisle end display
National Brand			
Portfolio risk	-17%	+2%	+27%
Customer equity of new customers	-12%	+2%	+7%
Global customer equity	+4.1%	+0.8%	-10.6%
Private label brand			
Portfolio risk	-1%	0%	+1%
Customer equity of new customers	0%	+1%	0%
Global customer equity	+0.7%	+0.2%	-0.9%

pact on private label brands. H2 is validated too essentially for national brands (impact of non-monetary promotions on new CE between +2% and +7%) but even for private label brands (impact between 0% and +1%). H3 is rejected: monetary promotions increase the global CE (+0.7%). H4 (positive impact of non-monetary promotions on global CE) is validated for leaflets and rejected for aisle end displays. H5 is validated: promotions have a stronger impact on the global CE of brands with strong brand equity.

4 Discussion, implications and research directions

Our conclusions on the efficiency of promotions are slightly different from existing literature. Firstly, monetary promotions are overall very positive in the long term (i.e. on the CE), contrary to a large portion of literature (Jedidi et al, 1999; Mela et al, 1997). Conversely, the role of non-monetary promotions is questioned, which is not the dominant conclusion of existing literature (Sriram et al, 2007). Non-monetary promotions degrade the products' sign value, at least in the case of aisle end displays. In any case, their positive impact remains limited. This rejection is as strong as the brand is strong, which is in keeping with the theory.

The methodological contribution of this article lies in a shift from measuring the effects on sales to long-term evaluation through customer equity. The introduction of explanatory variables in purely stochastic models marks a technical and conceptual improvement. From a conceptual point of view, the introduction of explanatory variables allows to make possible the estimation of a behavioral impact of marketing actions. In managerial terms, our research showed that the most complex models could be implemented on panel data widely used by managers. All marketing actions must be evaluated as part of a customer portfolio in relation to profitability and risk.

Our research contains several limitations. Firstly, the external validity of our research is limited: only two brands, the retail sector and no competitors' reactions. Secondly, the magnitude of the monetary promotions is not illustrated by our definition. Finally, the informational prerequisites of NBD models mean that explanatory variables lack a dynamic perspective.

References

Abe M (2009a) "Counting Your Customers" one by one: A hierarchical bayes extension to the Pareto/NBD model. Marketing Science 28(3):541–553

Abe M (2009b) Customer lifetime value and RFM data: Accounting your customers: One by one. CIRJE F-Series CIRJE-F-616, CIRJE, Faculty of Economics, University of Tokyo

Blattberg RC, Neslin S (1990) Sales Promotion, Concepts, Methods and Strategies. Prentice Hall, Englewood Cliffs, NJ

Castéran H, Meyer-Waarden L, C B (2007) Incorporating covariates into the Pareto/NBD model: An empirical comparison of alternative lifetime value models. In: German-French-Austrian Conference on Quantitative Marketing. ESSEC

Fader P, Hardie B (2007) Incorporating time-invariant covariates into the Pareto/NBD and BG/NBD models, working paper, available at http://brucehardie.com/notes/019/

Fader P, Hardie B (2010) Customer-base valuation in a contractual setting: The perils of ignoring heterogeneity. Marketing Science 29(1):85–93

Fader P, Hardie B, Lee KL (2005a) "Counting your Customers" the easy way: An alternative to the Pareto/NBD model. Marketing Science 24(2):275–284

Fader P, Hardie B, Lee KL (2005b) RFM and CLV: Using iso-value curves
    for customer base analysis. Journal of Marketing Research 42(4):415–
    430
Gupta S, Hanssens D, Hardie B, Kahn W, Kumar V, Lin N, Ravishanker
    N, Sriram S (2006) Modeling customer lifetime value. Journal of Ser-
    vice Research 9(2):139–155, DOI 10.1177/1094670506293810
Helsen K, Schmittlein D (1992) How does a product market's typical
    price-promotion pattern affect the timing of households' purchases?
    an empirical study using upc scanner data. Journal of Retailing
    68(3):316–338
Jedidi K, Mela C, Gupta S (1999) Managing advertising and promotion
    for long-run profitability. Marketing Science 18(1):1–22
Mela CF, Gupta S, Lehmann D (1997) The long-term impact of promo-
    tion and advertising on consumer brand choice. Journal of Marketing
    Research 34(2):248–261
Slotegraaf RJ, Pauwels K (2008) The impact of brand equity and innova-
    tion on the long-term effectiveness of promotions. Journal of Marketing
    Research 45(3):293–306
Sriram S, Balachander S, Kalwani M (2007) Monitoring the dynamics of
    brand equity using store-level data. Journal of Marketing 71(2):61–78
Van Heerde HJ, Leeflang P, Wittink D (2004) Decomposing the sales pro-
    motion bump with store data. Marketing Science 23(3):317–334

The "Pay What You Want" Pricing Policy: Power Sharing or Communication Action?

Sihem Dekhili and Chantal Connan Ghesquiere

Abstract The academic literature focusing on consumer empowerment has studied the issue of the product (co-creation, co-innovation), the brand (brand community, consumers' tributes), the communication (lead users) and the consumer work. However, it is surprising to note that little attention has been given to the consumer participation to price setting, and particularly to the "Pay What You Want (PWYW)" pricing mechanism. Although researchers do not examine this issue, a number of enterprises have adopted this new pricing policy.

Recently, several reports and newspaper articles have largely evoked this subject by describing it as innovative and as a marketing tool (remedy to the purchasing power crisis, setting a fair price, regaining customers ...). The aim of this study is to explore the PWYW mechanism: Is it a communication tool as mentioned by the media or a new participative mechanism which enables power sharing between the enterprise and its customers?

We are interested in the enterprises' point of view and we hope to identify the reasons which can explain why managers take the risk to decrease

Sihem Dekhili
HuManiS (EA 1347), EM Strasbourg Business School – University of Strasbourg – 61, avenue de la Forêt Noire - 67085 Strasbourg Cedex, France,
✉ sihem.dekhili@em-strasbourg.eu

Chantal Connan Ghesquiere
HuManiS (EA 1347), EM Strasbourg Business School – University of Strasbourg
✉ ch.ghesquiere@gmail.com

CUSTOMER & SERVICE SYSTEMS
KIT SCIENTIFIC PUBLISHING
Vol. 1, No. 1, S. 25–29, 2014

DOI 10.5445/KSP/1000038784/03
ISSN 2198-8005

their profits. The intention of the enterprise is it really to more involve customers in the decision making?

1 Theoretical Framework

The development of the Internet and Web 2.0 has changed the relationship between the company and the consumer (Fuchs et al, 2010). Consequently, managers have adopted the empowerment principles (Prahalad and Ramaswamy, 2000) to offer their customers the opportunity to express their opinions and to participate in the general offer design (Ramani and Kumar, 2008). The mechanism of empowerment requires measures allowing consumers to intervene on several variables of the marketing mix, and companies to use the consumers' skills (Bonnemaizon et al, 2008).

The power asymmetry between the customer and the enterprise is rebalancing, consumers are participating in the decision making (Cova and Ezan, 2008). They are aware that they can influence the enterprise' outcome. Therefore, final decisions become their "own" decisions which generate positive emotions among consumers. These feelings could increase the perceived value of the good and create a stronger involvement of the customer.

Nobody could imagine that the consumer may intervene in the price setting of a good, except in the case of trade negotiations that have always existed between a seller and a customer. Nonetheless, the consumer has participated in this task through several mechanisms such as auctions, the "Name Your Own Price (NYOP)" and the "Pay What You Want (PWYW)". If in the two first cases, the buyer sets the final price, the PWYW mechanism gives to consumer the highest level of power (Kim et al, 2009). While in the NYOP case, the seller sets a threshold below which he refuses the consumer's offer, however in the PWYW case, no threshold is established.

The PWYW pricing policy tends to create a different kind of relationship between the seller and the customer which extends the only commercial and monetary exchange by a social dimension. The commercial relationship can be based on other foundations (responsibility, confidence) than the financial gain. The PWYW presents advantages for the enterprise: differentiate the enterprise from the competition, attract new customers, generate free advertising, increase the notoriety, reduce the price unfairness, explore the customers willingness to pay. Through this mechanism, the enterprise can expect to increase customers' loyalty and create a positive social image.

Despite this list of advantages, the PWYW is usually associated with an evident risk related to the consumers' abuse. However, the study of Kim et al (2009) shows that in the PWYW case, consumers are not always motivated by the maximization of their utility. Their behaviors are also guided by social rules and they consider fairness towards the seller.

2 Method and Result

We analyzed forty newspaper articles on the PWYW issue. This primary work enabled us to develop the interview guideline used in the second part of the research. We conducted twelve telephone interviews with heads of organizations that have practiced at least once the PWYW pricing policy. The interview guideline consisted of questions, essentially about the explanation of pricing mechanism principles, the managers' motivations, the link between the adopted strategy and the propensity to involve the consumer in the organization decisions, the consumers' behaviors and reactions.

Our results show that the motivations of the managers interviewed are not always participatory or mercantile in nature. The contributions of respondents allowed us to classify them into two groups.

The first group of managers focused on a relational approach which is characterized by sharing and solidarity principles. The PWYW mechanism consists in this case in creating exchange opportunities with customers. It allows more people to access services or products unaffordable for them in normal circumstances. This approach seems to meet the social marketing perspective. The second group perceives the PWYW as an opportunity to talk about enterprises at a low cost of communication, attract new customers or increase sales during some periods.

Managers naively thought that customers would all pay a price close to the usual one. They do not measure the extent of the power they gave to consumers and were perhaps not ready to accept a new form of governance. We observed that some managers had limited the possibilities of consumers in setting prices, which is in contradiction with the PWYW principle. For this, they implemented some specific actions: restrict the operation to a part of the enterprise's activities and intervene at the time of payment.

The enterprise is not the only one to reject this new participative process, the accustomed consumers seem to be reluctant, they feel responsible for the survival of the firm and think they have to pay the usual price. These results underline some customers' resistance toward the PWYW process and point out the importance of loyalty for the price setting process by consumers. This is especially emphasized in the case of restaurant case which is characterized by a strong (face to face) interaction between the consumer and the seller (Kim et al, 2009).

Studies focusing on the issue of customer empowerment highlight the interest in marketing based on customer's knowledge and expertise (Bonnemaizon et al, 2008). In most cases, customer's expertise is challenged by the manager who is scared of a customer who does not pay the right price because of opportunism or incompetence. Price setting in PWYW's field may be a complicated practice for the customer.

The last result shows that although the PWYW concept seems to be profitable for the enterprise (Kim et al, 2009), none of the respondents says clearly that the action was beneficial, most of the managers interviewed express some fears linked to the financial risk. However, we deduced from the discourse analysis that the operation was profitable.

3 Conclusion

The PWYW interest can be double for the enterprise:

1. To get information (how does the consumer perceive the product, what price is he willing to pay, what kind of adjustments can be made...);
2. To create and motivate a new exchange area between the manager and the consumer which favors customers' loyalty.

Promoting positive emotions linked to the price, through the PWYW, could be a solution to reinforce the trust between enterprises and consumers as well as to enhance the seller's credibility. In addition to the customers' desire to realize a good deal with PWYW, some people seem to appreciate to be involved into an innovative consumption experience.

Our research nevertheless displays some limitations which are important to keep in mind. The first concerns the size of the sample, the study is an exploratory one and its results may not be generalized. Another limitation relates to the respondents' answers. This study tackles a sensitive issue for managers: the price issue and enterprises profit. It is possible to imagine that some managers did not feel free to answer our questions. Finally, the current study has been limited to the managers' point of view. We believe it would be fruitful for future research to explore also the consumers' perception of the PWYW mechanism.

References

Bonnemaizon A, Curbatov O, Louyot-Gallicher M (2008) Le knowledge marketing, une voie applicative du customer empowerment. In: International Congress of Marketing Trends, Venice, vol 7

Cova B, Ezan P (2008) Le consommateur-collaborateur: Activités, attentes et impacts. Le cas du passionné de warhammer. In: Journées de recherche en marketing de Bourgogne, Dijon, vol 13

Fuchs C, Prandelli E, Schreier M (2010) The psychological effects of empowerment strategies on consumers' product demand. Journal of Marketing 74(1):65–79

Kim JY, Martin N, Spann M (2009) Pay what you want: A new participative pricing mechanism. Journal of Marketing 73(1):44–58

Prahalad CK, Ramaswamy V (2000) Co-opting customer competence. Harvard Business Review 78(1):79–87

Ramani G, Kumar V (2008) Interaction orientation and firm performance. Journal of Marketing 72(1):27–45

How Profound Is the Allure of Endowed Status in Hierarchical Loyalty Programs?

Andreas Eggert, Ina Garnefeld and Lena Steinhoff

Abstract Hierarchical loyalty programs are common relationship marketing instruments that award elevated status to customers exceeding a certain spending level (e.g., gold membership, platinum customer). In business practice, some companies also offer elevated status to selected customers even if they do not meet the required spending level, in an attempt to profit from the profound allure of status. Relying on social psychology research, this study analyzes the loyalty impact of such a status endowment. A first experimental study reveals the bright and dark sides of endowed status, with customer gratitude and customer skepticism acting as mediating mechanisms. A second experiment delineates that in order to alleviate the dark side, managers should let target customers make an active choice to be endowed with status and select target customers who are close to achieving that status on their own.

Andreas Eggert
University of Paderborn, Marketing Department, Paderborn, Germany,
✉ andreas.eggert@wiwi.upb.de

Ina Garnefeld
Bergische University Wuppertal, Schumpeter School of Business and Economics, Service Management Department, Wuppertal, Germany,
✉ garnefeld@wiwi.uni-wuppertal.de

Lena Steinhoff
University of Paderborn, Marketing Department, Paderborn, Germany,
✉ lena.steinhoff@wiwi.upb.de

CUSTOMER & SERVICE SYSTEMS
KIT SCIENTIFIC PUBLISHING
Vol. 1, No. 1, S. 31–36, 2014

DOI 10.5445/KSP/1000038784/04
ISSN 2198-8005

1 Introduction

In hierarchical loyalty programs, firms reward customers not only on the basis of their repeat purchasing (Kivetz and Simonson, 2002) but also according to whether they exceed certain spending levels (Meyer-Waarden, 2007; Meyer-Waarden and Benavent, 2009; Wagner et al, 2009). Awarding elevated status to a customer can provide the firm with increased customer loyalty (e.g. Drèze and Nunes, 2011; Lacey et al, 2007; Meyer-Waarden, 2013) and stronger alignment of the costs to serve a customer with his or her value to the firm (Kumar and Reinartz, 2006). Hierarchical loyalty programs thus appear in many different industries, including airlines (e.g., American Airlines AAdvantage), hotels (e.g., Hilton HHonors), and credit cards (e.g., American Express Centurion).

Some companies further award customers elevated status even before they achieve the spending level predefined in the loyalty program's rules. Thus, certain customers who typically are expected to be of high value for the firm but are still in the basic tier of a hierarchical loyalty program are elevated to a higher tier, without having met the spending level required for status elevation (Kumar and Shah, 2004). In this case, the elevated status is endowed rather than achieved, because its attainment is beyond customers' control (Drèze and Nunes, 2009). We find several examples of companies that endow such elevated status, including Accor Hotels (A|Club), Starwood Hotels & Resorts (Starwood Preferred Guest), or Hertz Car Rental (Hertz Gold Plus Rewards).

Status endowment might be profitable if firms attain loyalty effects similar to those caused by awarding achieved status. However, using social psychology research, we argue that endowment differs from achievement in its impact on customer loyalty. Specifically, endowed status should entail both bright and dark side effects. On the one hand, endowed elevated status can initiate a loyalty-enhancing effect through customer gratitude. On the other hand, though, endowed elevated status might result in customer skepticism and thereby bring about a loyalty-reducing effect. We further suggest that the dark side effect depends on the specific endowment design, such that companies should be able to manage the extent to which customer skepticism arises. Designing status endowment in a way that fosters customers' perceptions of control and eligibility, managers can help reduce skepticism.

Analyzing the phenomenon of endowed elevated customer status thus has key implications for the management of hierarchical loyalty programs. Understanding its impact on customer loyalty might help managers evaluate the efficacy of endowed status as an instrument for effectively prioritizing valuable customers and managing their loyalty.

2 Study 1: The Bright and Dark Sides of Status Endowment in Hierarchical Loyalty Programs

In Study 1, to analyze the effectiveness of status endowment for increasing customer loyalty, we take both potential positive and potential negative psychological mechanisms into consideration. We compare being endowed with an elevated customer status against not receiving such elevated status, as well as with the regular achievement of elevated status.

Based on social identity theory (Tajfel and Turner, 1986) and the concept of gratitude-based reciprocity (Palmatier et al, 2009), we assume endowed status to initiate a loyalty-enhancing effect via customer gratitude. However, referring to attribution theory (Weiner, 1985) and the persuasion knowledge model (Friestad and Wright, 1994), we also propose endowed status to result in a loyalty-reducing effect via customer skepticism. Comparing endowed with achieved status, we suggest endowed status to foster skepticism and thereby entail a dark side that does not occur for achieved status.

In our experiment, we employed a posttest control group design and manipulated customer status on three levels (endowed versus achieved versus no elevated customer status). A total of 221 participants took part in the experiment. The mean age of the sample was 33.1 years and 53.3% were female. Our results show the proposed bright and dark side loyalty effects: Via gratitude, endowed status increases loyalty. Via skepticism, endowed status decreases loyalty. As compared to achieved status, endowed status reduces loyalty by generating skepticism.

3 Study 2: Alleviating the Dark Side with Status Endowment Design Characteristics

In Study 2, we seek insight into the use of different design characteristics of status endowment offerings as potential ways to decrease the skepticism perceived by customers when being endowed with elevated status.

We propose that designing a status endowment in a way that gives customers a sense of control over the endowment will decrease customer skepticism, as explained by attribution theory (Weiner, 1985). In particular, we suggest customers' freedom of choice and their proximity to status achievement to convert solely external to partly internal attribution. Both design characteristics serve as means to reduce customer skepticism and enhance customer loyalty.

Our experiment used a 2 × 2 between-subjects factorial design in which we manipulated the freedom of choice (active versus no active choice) and the proximity to status achievement (high versus low proximity). In total, 284 participants took part in the experiment. Our sample had a mean age of 32.5 years and 50.5% of respondents were female. Results reveal customer skepticism-alleviating effects of both customers' freedom of choice and their proximity to status achievement, which indirectly increase customer loyalty.

4 Discussion and Implications

Demonstrating the differential loyalty effects of status endowment has three major implications. First, our simultaneous consideration of the bright and dark side loyalty effects of endowed status reveals that both influences cancel each other out, making status endowment ineffective for driving customer loyalty. These findings underscore the importance of considering the dark sides of relationship marketing investments on the focal customer. Customers might interpret companies' activities as self-interested persuasion attempts.

Second, the bright side effect of endowed status on customer loyalty implies that awarding customers elevated status, even though they did not achieve it, can be an effective means for enhancing their loyalty. Managers of hierarchical loyalty programs can employ the general appeal of status (Henderson et al, 2011) as a stimulus to generate gratitude and motivate customers toward greater loyalty.

Third, endowed status possesses a dark side too, and managers must take care when elevating customers' status through endowment, because it can foster skepticism. Status endowment should not be designed as a "pure" endowment. Rather, it should be carried out in a way that augments customers' perceptions of personal choice or achievement to foster effectiveness.

References

Drèze X, Nunes JC (2009) Feeling superior: The impact of loyalty program structure on consumers' perceptions of status. Journal of Consumer Research 35(6):890–905

Drèze X, Nunes JC (2011) Recurring goals and learning: The impact of successful reward attainment on purchase behavior. Journal of Marketing Research 48(2):268–281

Friestad M, Wright P (1994) The persuasion knowledge model: How people cope with persuasion attempts. Journal of Consumer Research 21(1):1–31

Henderson CM, Beck JT, Palmatier RW (2011) Review of the theoretical underpinnings of loyalty programs. Journal of Consumer Psychology 21(3):256–276

Kivetz R, Simonson I (2002) Earning the right to indulge: Effort as a determinant of customer preferences toward frequency program rewards. Journal of Marketing Research 39(2):155–170

Kumar V, Reinartz WJ (2006) Customer relationship management: A databased approach. Wiley, Hoboken, NJ

Kumar V, Shah D (2004) Building and sustaining profitable customer loyalty for the 21st century. Journal of Retailing 80(4):317–330

Lacey R, Suh J, Morgan RM (2007) Differential effects of preferential treatment levels on relational outcomes. Journal of Service Research 9(3):241–256

Meyer-Waarden L (2007) The effects of loyalty programs on customer lifetime duration and share of wallet. Journal of Retailing 83(2):223–236, DOI 10.1016/j.jretai.2007.01.002

Meyer-Waarden L (2013) The impact of reward personalisation on frequent flyer programmes' perceived value and loyalty. Journal of Services Marketing 27(3):183–194, DOI 10.1108/08876041311330681

Meyer-Waarden L, Benavent C (2009) Grocery retail loyalty program effects: self-selection or purchase behavior change? Journal of the Academy of Marketing Science 37(3):345–358, DOI 10.1007/s11747-008-0123-z

Meyer-Waarden L, Benavent C, Castéran H (2014) The impact of loyalty programs' gratifications on purchase behavior according to purchasing strategies. International Journal of Retail and Distribution Management forthcoming

Palmatier RW, Jarvis C, Bechkoff JR, Kardes FR (2009) The role of customer gratitude in relationship marketing. Journal of Marketing 73(5):1–18

Tajfel H, Turner JC (1986) The social identity theory of intergroup behavior. In: Worchel S, Austin LW (eds) Psychology of Intergroup Relations, Nelson-Hall, Chicago, pp 7–24

Wagner T, Hennig-Thurau T, Rudolph T (2009) Does customer demotion jeopardize loyalty? Journal of Marketing 73(3):69–85

Weiner B (1985) An attributional theory of achievement motivation and emotion. Psychological Review 92(4):548–573

Recent Advances in Modularity Optimization and Their Application in Retailing

Andreas Geyer-Schulz and Michael Ovelgönne

Abstract   In this contribution we report on three recent advances in modularity optimization, namely:

1. The randomized greedy (RG) family of modularity optimization algorithms are state-of-the-art graph clustering algorithms which are near optimal, fast, and scalable.
2. The extension of the RG family to multi-level clustering.
3. A new entropy based cluster index which allows the detection of the proper clustering levels and of stable core clusters at each level.

Last, but not least, several marketing applications of these algorithms for customer enablement and empowerment are discussed: e.g. the detection of low-level cluster structures from retail purchase data, the analysis of the co-usage structure of scientific documents for detecting multi-level category structures for scientific libraries, and the analysis of social groups from the friend relation of social network sites.

Andreas Geyer-Schulz
Informationsdienste und elektronische Märkte, Karlsruhe Institute of Technology (KIT), Karlsruhe
✉ andreas.geyer-schulz@kit.edu

Michael Ovelgönne
UMIACS, University of Maryland, College Park, MD
✉ mov@umiacs.umd.edu

CUSTOMER & SERVICE SYSTEMS
KIT SCIENTIFIC PUBLISHING
Vol. 1, No. 1, S. 37–48, 2014

DOI 10.5445/KSP/1000038784/05
ISSN 2198-8005

1 The RG Family of Algorithms

In this section we give a short presentation of the RG family of algorithms which optimize the modularity measure introduced by Newman and Girvan (2004):

$$Q(G,C) = \sum_{i=1}^{p} (e_{ii} - a_i^2) \tag{1}$$

with $e_{ij} = \frac{\sum_{v_x \in C_i} \sum_{v_y \in C_j} m_{xy}}{\sum_{v_x \in V} \sum_{v_y \in V} m_{xy}}$ and $a_i = \sum_j e_{ij}$, where $G = (V, E)$ is a loop-free graph and $C = \{C_1, \ldots, C_p\}$ is a partition of V and M is the adjacency matrix of G defined by $m_{xy} = m_{yx} = 1$ if $\{v_x, v_y\} \in E$ and 0 otherwise.

Ovelgönne et al (2010a) and Ovelgönne and Geyer-Schulz (2010) modified Newman's greedy algorithm (Newman, 2004) by randomizing the selection of the first join candidate and by restricting the search for the second join candidate to the neighboring clusters of the first candidate. The randomized greedy (RG) algorithm accepts the best local improvement and, if no local improvement after k repetitions can be found, it accepts the join with the least decrease in modularity (like a walksat algorithm). The effect of the randomization of the greedy algorithm is dramatic: In the 10th DIMACS Implementation Challenge (2012), the RG algorithm won the Pareto challenge and is currently the most efficient graph-clustering algorithm. The main reason for the efficiency of the randomization lies in the large number of equivalence classes of joins with the same increase in modularity in real data sets (Ovelgönne and Geyer-Schulz, 2012a).

A greedy algorithm – even with the modifications described above – always finds a local optimum only. Ovelgönne and Geyer-Schulz (2012b) and Geyer-Schulz and Ovelgönne (2013) introduced a second idea to find heuristics which lead to better optima in modularity maximization: the core group graph clustering (CGGC) scheme. The CGGC scheme combines the locally optimal solutions found by several runs of the RG algorithm (or any other modularity optimization algorithm) in such a way that all the vertices which are in the same cluster in all locally optimal solutions form a core group. The result of this is a core group partition. The clusters of a core group partition contain the elements which have been in the same cluster in all locally optimal partitions the core group partition has been built from. Geyer-Schulz and Ovelgönne (2013) and

Ovelgönne and Geyer-Schulz (2013) characterize the core group partition as a saddle point on a Morse graph. Since a saddle point is always a point from which several local optima can be reached, saddle points are good restart points for an ensemble learning algorithm. The CGGC scheme may be used repeatedly, we denote this variant as CGGCi.

The ensemble algorithm based on a combination of the RG algorithm and the CGGC scheme won the modularity quality challenge of the 10th DIMACS Implementation Challenge (2012) and currently is the algorithm with the highest modularity for large graphs (e.g. 1.3 million vertices, 14 million edges). Computing time ranges from approximately 30 seconds (RG) to 9 minutes (CGGCi/RG) on standard PCs for a graph with approximately 860 000 vertices and 16 130 000 edges. A recent benchmark of implementations of the randomized greedy algorithm in five different programming languages (C++, Java, C#, F#, and Python) has appeared in Stein and Geyer-Schulz (2013). For additional results, see Ovelgönne and Geyer-Schulz (2012b), Geyer-Schulz and Ovelgönne (2013), and Ovelgönne and Geyer-Schulz (2013).

Fortunato and Barthélemy (2007) showed the problem of the resolution limit of modularity clustering, namely that the number of clusters chosen by modularity based graph clustering algorithms is approximately the square root of the number of edges. The second implication of the resolution limit is that modularity clustering favors partitions with clusters of equal size. To eliminate the resolution limit from modularity clustering (Geyer-Schulz et al, 2013) introduce a link parametrized modularity function with the parameter λ replacing the number of edges in the graph:

$$Q(G,C,\lambda) = \sum_{i=1}^{p} \left(\frac{l_i}{\lambda} - \left(\frac{d_i}{2\lambda} \right)^2 \right) = \frac{1}{\lambda} \sum_{i=1}^{p} \left(l_i - \frac{d_i^2}{4\lambda} \right) \qquad (2)$$

where l_i is the number of edges in cluster C_i and $d_i = 2l_i + l_i^{out}$ with l_i^{out} defined as the number of edges connecting vertices in C_i with vertices in the rest of the graph. For $\lambda \leq 4$ we get the singleton partition (the size of C_i is 1) and for $\lambda >> 4L$ we get a single cluster which contains the whole graph. This modification is the basis for using the RG-family of algorithms for multi-level clustering. Note, that the second implication of the resolution limit is still in place: The parametrized modularity function still favors partitions with clusters of approximately equal size.

2 Recognizing Clusters

Last, but not least, there remains the open problem of assessing the quality of a partition of vertices produced by a graph clustering algorithm. Since assessing the quality of a cluster partition by human experts which is still the gold standard in many areas of data analysis is impossible because of the sheer size of the graphs becoming available from Internet data sources, the proper evaluation of the result of clustering algorithms has become a major research problem. A common formal approach to this problem is to repeatedly apply a clustering algorithm and to assess the stability of the solution by measuring the similarity of pairs of the produced partitions and to evaluate the distribution of the similarities. The measures suggested can be classified as classical measures (e.g the Jaccard or the adjusted RAND index), set matching measures, and information based metrics. Two recent surveys on such measures are Meilă (2007) and Vinh et al (2010).

The key problem of this approach is that the similarity is assessed only between pairs of partitions and that the symmetries in solution sets are not properly respected: Consider e.g. a ring structure of n vertices. A modularity optimization algorithm will divide the ring in $\sqrt{n}$ clusters with $\sqrt{n}$ vertices – or as near as possible if n is not a square number. However, the partition we get will depend on the randomly selected starting point. And, of course, there exist n starting points and thus we may get n different partitions. Consequently, the ring structure has no cluster structure. However, measuring the similarity of pairs of partitions may not detect this.

Geyer-Schulz et al (2013) propose a new information measure to assess the information in a set of partitions. The basic idea of the measure is the following fact: Graph symmetries give rise to permutation groups: e.g. for a 9-element ring the permutation (912345678) is the generator of a automorphism group of the graph of this ring.

Let $Aut_s(P)$ be the set of all partitions generated from partition P by applying all permutations in the automorphism subgroup of graph G to partition P.

The information content of each vertex v is given by

$$H(v) = \min_{l \in L} H(v,l) = -\sum_{i=1}^{p} P(i,v,l)\log_2 P(i,v,l) \qquad (3)$$

where p is the number of clusters and $P(i,v)$ the probability that vertex v is in cluster C_i labelled l_i for all $Aut_s(P)$. L is the set of all possible ways to label the clusters in the partitions in P. The information content of vertices can be used to identify vertices which belong to a cluster (stable core groups) and vertices whose cluster membership changes.

The total entropy for the set of partitions $Aut_s(P)$ is then simply $H(Aut_s(P)) = \sum_{v \in V} H(v)$. This measure still depends on the choice of the assignment of vertices to clusters. To make the measure unique, we select the assignment of vertices to clusters which minimizes $H(Aut_s(P))$. And for partitions of regular graph structures like a ring, the entropy will be maximal, if the set of partitions we have used is $Aut_s(P)$. The last condition also indicates the main weakness of the proposed measures, namely the missing capability to efficiently compute $Aut_s(P)$.

3 Customer Empowerment, Customer Enablement and Modularity Clustering

Bowen and Lawler (1992) require that empowerment of service employees must be complemented by enabling service employees by management support, knowledge support, and technical support, so that empowerment works. The same holds for customer empowerment: Customer empowerment will only work, if customers are also enabled. And enablement of the customer depends on customer-oriented service processes. Critical for the success of such services is the development of a proper theoretical framework for each concrete service which spans the gap between marketing and computer science.

In the following we present three scenarios in which we highlight the potential of the RG family of modularity clustering algorithms for implementing innovative customer-oriented service processes.

The first scenario is a retail scenario: Recently (Die Zeit, 19.12.2012 (Schadwinkel, 2012c,a,b)), several retailers (and direct marketers) offer the time-buying customer (Berry, 1979) new services like "the menu in the bag" (Perfetto, Karstadt), "the walk-through receipt book" (Kochhaus, Hamburg and Berlin) and "the delivered menu" (KommtEssen, Kochzauber, KochAbo, Schlemmertüte, HelloFresh). What the customer buys, is a bundle of complementary products (the ingredients of the menu (more or less preprocessed) in the proper weight ratio) together with a process description for cooking the menu.

Even a rather crude value analysis of these menu services (see e.g. Anderson et al (2006)) reveals that customer benefits are not restricted to time savings, but that a rather subtle picture of consumer benefits exists: The bundle of complementary products in one bag eliminates the search for menu ingredients (and the uncertainty of choice in combining ingredients). Preprocessed ingredients reduce the number of preprocessing steps (washing, cooking, blending, cutting to shape, ...) and the time needed for them. Packing ingredients in the proper weight ratio eliminates weighing (and errors in weighing) and reduces losses from excess ingredients caused by unfitting package sizes and the effort of waste reduction by proper menu sequencing. Eliminating the need for menu sequencing reduces the consumer's constraints in menu selection. Finally, a proper process description eliminates the search for the cooking receipt and eliminates uncertainty and potential pitfalls in the cooking process. Process descriptions, of course, can be multi-media based and distributed via mobile and/or social media (e.g. cooking video clips on YouTube).

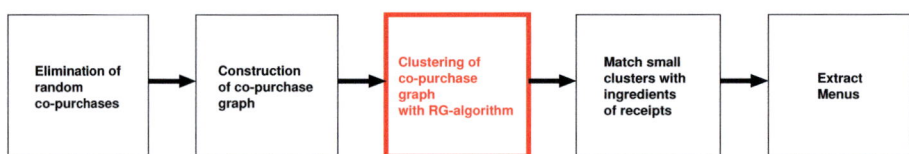

Fig. 1 The data analysis process for menu services

The micro-economic background theory for these services is the analysis of complementarities (induced by receipts as technological production functions) as presented e.g. in (Milgrom and Roberts, 1992, pp. 106-113). Clearly, analysing complementarities in a retailer's sortiment is a promising application of RG algorithms (and of Ehrenberg's repeat-buying theory (see Ehrenberg (1988)), a classic quantitative marketing theory): Figure 1 shows a generic 5-step data analysis process for supporting this type of service from a retailer's point of view:

1. The data source are market baskets from POS scanner data. In this preprocessing step random co-purchases are eliminated with the help of Ehrenberg's logarithmic series models (see Böhm et al (2003)).

2. Next, an unweighted co-purchase graph is constructed from the non-random co-purchases generated in the previous step.

3. The unweighted co-purchase graph is clustered with the RG algorithm or one of its variants. For the innovative retail services discussed above a scale transformation of the cluster criterium (see formula 2) which produces relatively small clusters must be found. In addition, stable clusters must be identified with the help of the methods presented in section 2.

4. These clusters are matched with the ingredient list of a large recipe data base to identify popular menus which are candidates to be offered by such services.

5. The candidate menus are evaluated with regard to their potential margin contributions, popularity, the availability of the basic ingredients and the capacity of the prepackaging facility. Finally, the menus satisfying the retailer's profitability and availability criteria are selected and extracted.

The second scenario is the analysis of the co-usage structure of scientific documents. Data sources are Google Scholar or the BibTip GmbH (http://www.bibtip.com), a small German scientific recommender service provider. BibTip currently has recommender information on 150 million scientific documents with a growth rate of approximately 1.3 million transactions per day. The preprocessing step corresponds to the first subprocess in the first scenario.

However, in this scenario, the theoretical justification of the data analysis performed rests on the economic principles of incentive compatibility and self-selection (see (Milgrom and Roberts, 1992, pp. 140-146 and pp. 154-158) and Spence (1974)). Time pressures on researchers as well as students lead to incentive compatibility in information search: Almost all of the users of a scientific library conduct their literature search task-specific and as efficiently as possible. As a consequence, their choice behavior truthfully reflects their search interests and the search logs record their true behavior (incentive compatibility). The task-specific nature of the search behavior leads to self-selection: Users choosing the same information object have similar search interests and perform similar research tasks. This self-selection effect allows the transfer of Ehrenberg's repeat-buying theory to the analysis of anonymous session data and the identification of recommendations: All anonymous market baskets which contain the same information object are considered as the purchase history of a latent, locally homogenous cluster of users whose revealed preferences (by their choices) are recorded, aggregated, and analyzed. The privacy of the user is respected. The results of the preprocessing step are the basis of BibTip's recommender service (Geyer-Schulz et al, 2003).

Construction of a recommender graph and clustering of the recommender graph can be done by the RG family of algorithms. Multi-level clusters can be exploited for an improvement of the categorization of scientific documents, since currently only about 12 percent of scientific documents are properly tagged in the German scientific library system. Prototypes of new user interfaces which enable the user to navigate on the recommendation network and thus through a semantic knowledge network have already been built (Neumann et al, 2008). Additional analysis options may include the automatic analysis of knowledge diffusion and knowledge transfer.

A direct application of social network analysis techniques for the purpose of analysing information needs, information exposure, information legitimation, information routes, and information opportunities as promoted e.g. by (Haythornthwaite, 1996) requires the observation of information and communication flows between scientists and students. Monitoring information and communication flows, however, is a violation of the privacy of users and of data protection laws in most countries. Librarians strongly oppose this type of system instrumentation. However, a qualitative analysis of the information flows in a university environment reveals that a strengthening of the information routes from the most experienced and advanced researchers in a disciplines to the novice students is desirable. A prototype of such a system (myVU) based on pseudo-identities and self-assessment of experience had been implemented and deployed in a university environment by (Geyer-Schulz et al, 2001). However, user acceptance and support for this system was rather low. The introduction of role-based extensions of scientific recommender systems has failed because of privacy concerns. The challenge in introducing even moderately personalized information systems is to do it in a privacy-aware manner which is accepted by users.

The third scenario is the identification of social groups from the friendship link relation of social network sites like Facebook, Google+, or Xing. In this setting, no preprocessing is necessary, the RG algorithms can be directly applied to the complete friendship graph. However, depending on the application, partitions of clusters with appropriate size (corresponding to social groups at different scales) have to be selected. Doing this in a proper way remains difficult without additional data enrichment because of the trend to have considerably more friends in the Internet than in real life. At least for the network provider, data enrichment by attributes from personal profiles, additional communication data, etc. is an option. A first application scenario of social clustering for emergency alerts which is based on the social psychological analysis of bystander behavior has been described by Geyer-Schulz et al (2010), Ovelgönne et al (2010b), and Geyer-Schulz et al (2012). Again, the theoretical backing for this scenario is rather intricate: Darley and Latané provided a careful analysis of bystander behavior in emergencies (see Latané and Darley (1970)) which has been verified by social psychological experiments over the next 25 years (for a recent survey see Brehm et al (2005)). The key finding of Darley and Latané (and their followers) is that a victim in an emergency is more likely to receive help if at least a weak social tie with one bystander exists. This finding provides the link to Granovetter's theory of the role of weak links in society (Granovetter, 1973) and to social clustering.

The exploration of social clustering for customer empowerment and enablement remains an important topic for further research. As the three examples given above show, the design of services for customer empowerment and enablement require a sound theoretical foundation.

References

Anderson JC, Narus JA, Rossum WV (2006) Customer value propositions in business markets. Harvard Business Review 84(3):91 – 99

Berry LL (1979) The time-buying consumer. Journal of Retailing 55(4):58–69

Böhm W, Geyer-Schulz A, Hahsler M, Jahn M (2003) Repeat-buying theory and its application for recommender services. In: Schwaiger M, Opitz O (eds) Exploratory Data Analysis in Empirical Research, Springer-Verlag, Heidelberg, Studies in Classification, Data Analysis, and Knowledge Organization, vol 22, pp 229 – 239

Bowen DE, Lawler EW (1992) The empowerment of service workers: What, why, how, and when. Sloan Management Review 33(3):31–39

Brehm SS, Kassin S, Fein S (2005) Social Psychology, 6th edn. Houghton Mifflin Company, Boston

Ehrenberg AS (1988) Repeat-Buying: Facts, Theory and Applications: Facts, Theory and Applications, 2nd edn. Charles Griffin & Company Ltd, London

Fortunato S, Barthélemy M (2007) Resolution limit in community detection. Proc National Academy of Sciences of the United States of America 104(1):36 – 41

Geyer-Schulz A, Ovelgönne M (2013) The randomized greedy modularity clustering algorithm and the core groups graph clustering scheme. In: Gaul W, Geyer-Schulz A, Okada A, Baba Y (eds) German-Japanese Interchange of Data Analysis Results, Springer, Heidelberg, Studies in Classification, Data Analysis, and Knowledge Organization, pp 15–34

Geyer-Schulz A, Hahsler M, Jahn M (2001) Educational and scientific recommender systems: Designing the information channels of the virtual university. International Journal of Engineering Education 17(2):153 – 163

Geyer-Schulz A, Neumann A, Thede A (2003) An architecture for behavior-based library recommender systems. Information Technology and Libraries 22(4):165 – 174

Geyer-Schulz A, Ovelgönne M, Sonnenbichler A (2010) Getting help in a crowd – a social emergency alert service. In: Institute for Systems and Technologies of Information, Control and Communication (ed) Proceedings of the International Conference on e-Business, Athens, Greece, pp 207–220

Geyer-Schulz A, Ovelgönne M, Sonnenbichler AC (2012) A social location-based emergency service to eliminate the bystander effect. In: MS Obaidat JF GA Tsihrintzis (ed) e-Business and Telecommunications, Communications in Computer and Information Science, vol 222, Springer Berlin / Heidelberg, pp 112 – 130

Geyer-Schulz A, Ovelgönne M, Stein M (2013) Modified randomized modularity clustering: Adapting the resolution limit. In: Lausen B, van den Poel D, Alfred U (eds) Algorithms from and for Nature and Life: Classification and Data Analysis, Springer, Heidelberg, Studies in Classification, Data Analysis, and Knowledge Organization, pp 355–364

Granovetter MS (1973) The strength of weak ties. The American Journal of Sociology 78(6):1360 – 1380

Haythornthwaite C (1996) Social network analysis: An approach and technique for the study of information exchange. Library & Information Science Research 18(4):323 – 342

Latané B, Darley J (1970) The Unresponsive Bystander: Why doesn't he help? Appleton-Century-Crofts, New York

Meilă M (2007) Comparing clusterings – an information based distance. Journal of Multivariate Analysis 98(5):873–895

Milgrom P, Roberts J (1992) Economics, Organization and Management, 1st edn. Prentice Hall

Neumann AW, Philipp M, Riedel F (2008) Recodiver: Browsing behavior-based recommendations on dynamic graphs. AI Communications 21(2-3):177 – 183

Newman MEJ (2004) Fast algorithm for detecting community structure in networks. Physical Review E 69(6):066,133

Newman MEJ, Girvan M (2004) Finding and evaluating community structure in networks. Physical Review E 69(2):026,113

Ovelgönne M, Geyer-Schulz A (2010) Cluster cores and modularity maximization. In: ICDMW '10. IEEE International Conference on Data Mining Workshops, Piscataway, pp 1204 – 1213

Ovelgönne M, Geyer-Schulz A (2012a) A comparison of agglomerative hierarchical algorithms for modularity clustering. In: Gaul W, Geyer-Schulz A, Schmidt-Thieme L, Kunze J (eds) Proceedings of the 34th Conference of the German Classification Society, Springer, Heidelberg, Studies in Classification, Data Analysis, and Knowledge Organization, pp 225 – 232

Ovelgönne M, Geyer-Schulz A (2012b) An ensemble-learning strategy for graph-clustering. In: Bader DA, Meyerhenke H, Sanders P, Wagner D (eds) 10th DIMACS Implementation Challenge – Graph Partitioning and Graph Clustering, Rutgers University, DIMACS – Center for Discrete Mathematics and Theoretical Computer Science, http://www.cc.gatech.edu/dimacs10/papers/[18]-dimacs10_ovelgoennegeyerschulz.pdf

Ovelgönne M, Geyer-Schulz A (2013) An ensemble learning strategy for graph clustering. In: Bader DA, Meyerhenke H, Sanders P, Wagner D (eds) Graph Partitioning and Graph Clustering, American Mathematical Society, Providence, Contemporary Mathematics, vol 588, pp 187–205

Ovelgönne M, Geyer-Schulz A, Stein M (2010a) Randomized greedy modularity optimization for group detection in huge social networks. 4th ACM SNA-KDD Workshop on Social Network Mining and Analysis 2010:1–9

Ovelgönne M, Sonnenbichler AC, Geyer-Schulz A (2010b) Social emergency alert service – a location-based privacy-aware personal safety service. In: Proceedings of the 2010 Fourth International Conference on Next Generation Mobile Applications, Services and Technologies, IEEE Computer Society, Los Alamitos, CA, USA, pp 84 – 89

Schadwinkel A (2012a) Begehbares Rezept. Die Zeit 2012(52):36

Schadwinkel A (2012b) Liefern statt kaufen. Die Zeit 2012(52):36

Schadwinkel A (2012c) Menü in der Tüte. Die Zeit 2012(52):36

Spence MA (1974) Market Signaling: Information Transfer in Hiring and Related Screening Processes. Harvard University Press, Cambridge, Massachusetts

Stein M, Geyer-Schulz A (2013) A comparison of five programming languages in a graph clustering scenario. Journal of Universal Computer Science 19(3):428 – 456

Vinh NX, Epps J, Bailey J (2010) Information theoretic measures for clusterings comparison: Variants, properties, normalization and correction for chance. J Mach Learn Res 11:2837–2854

Paying For a Higher Workload? The Relation Between Customer's Co-Production and Willingness to Pay

Nicola Bilstein, Jens Hogreve, Christina Sichtmann and René Fahr

We increasingly observe the use of co-production in managerial practice, as customers undertake additional tasks in service processes that service providers traditionally have performed. In 1995 Continental was the first airline to offer self-check-in kiosks, but today more than two thirds of travelers check in using self-service. Similarly, since their introduction more than 10 years ago, supermarket self-checkouts have grown widespread (Hill, 2011). Nor are these shifts to more customer co-production limited to technology-enabled contexts. Even some high-end restaurants use co-production as core part of their business model, such as the Seafood Market and Restaurant in Bangkok, where customers take a shopping trolley and wander around the market to choose their food. They move to the checkout counter, where it is weighed and sent to the kitchen while customers pay, before being seated to wait for their dishes (http://www.seafood.co.th). In all these examples,

Nicola Bilstein
Catholic University of Eichstaett-Ingolstadt,
✉ nicola.bilstein@ku.de

Jens Hogreve
Catholic University of Eichstaett-Ingolstadt
✉ jens.hogreve@ku.de

Christina Sichtmann
University of Vienna
✉ christina.sichtmann@univie.ac.at

René Fahr
University of Paderborn
✉ Rene.Fahr@wiwi.uni-paderborn.de

CUSTOMER & SERVICE SYSTEMS
KIT SCIENTIFIC PUBLISHING
Vol. 1, No. 1, S. 49–53, 2014

DOI 10.5445/KSP/1000038784/06
ISSN 2198-8005

providers benefit from co-production by substituting employee labor with customer efforts. This substitution can lead to productivity gains (Bendapudi and Leone, 2003).

Yet such productivity gains through co-production can be a double-edged sword. Acting as "partial" employees (Mills et al, 1983, p.120), customers might come to expect compensation for the time and effort they invest in the service process. Thus, co-production may reduce their willingness to pay (WTP), defined as the maximum price a customer will exchange (Wang et al, 2007) to receive a service they co-produce. In many cases, service firms compensate customers with a price reduction (e.g. Bowen, 1986), but if the price reduction must be very high to compensate customers, it might outweigh the company's productivity gains.

The price reductions offered for co-production often reflect the "gut feelings" of executives, who might award them without clear knowledge of whether and to what extent they are required by customers. Some customers simply do not expect any monetary compensation for their efforts, because in addition to inducing costs (i.e., efforts), co-production provides nonmonetary value (Yim et al, 2012). Customers might enjoy co-production and thus find value in it (Lusch et al, 2007); this value in turn can (partially) compensate customers and influence the relationship between their co-production and their WTP. This interaction requires managers to design pricing plans connected to co-production more carefully.

If the link between co-production and WTP is not as intuitive as it may seem at first, we consider it surprising that no empirical study has examined this relationship. To the best of our knowledge, this study offers the first empirical investigation of this issue, in an attempt to address three main research questions: Does co-production lead to lower or higher levels of WTP? To what extent does co-production decrease or increase WTP? Which factors moderate the link between co-production and WTP?

In turn, this research contributes to current research on co-production which represents one of the key topics in marketing and service research (Kunz and Hogreve, 2011). Prior studies link co-production to service quality, perceived control, enjoyment, satisfaction, well-being, and loyalty (e.g. Bendapudi and Leone, 2003; Gallan et al, 2013; Guo et al, 2013). Despite the relevance of this issue, the price-related consequences of co-production remain neglected; we extend previous research by linking co-production to customers' WTP. Beyond this main effect, we also provide evidence of the contingent nature of the relationship between co-production and WTP.

Definitions of co-production thus far have been neither selective nor consistent (e.g. Auh et al, 2007). The plethora of definitions has contributed to mixed and partly contradictory empirical results (Groth, 2005), though they all require customers to be active in the service process (e.g. Gallan et al, 2013). Because co-production processes vary with regard to the degree of customer participation, we also differentiate co-production activities that are inseparable from the customer (e.g., seeing the doctor for an examination) from those for which the performer does not matter (e.g., blow-drying hair at the hairdresser). These facets of co-production have not been discussed previously but seem highly relevant for effective co-production management. Specifically, co-production activities may have varying impacts on outcome variables such as WTP or satisfaction, depending on whether the customer must accomplish them or not. Non-transferable co-production involves activities that must be performed exclusively by customers. Transferable co-production instead refers to participative activities that can be delivered by the customer or the provider.

To address our central research questions, we conducted five studies regarding the relation of co-production with WTP and its moderators. We apply three methodological approaches. By relying on different experimental designs and using representative consumer and student data, we also affirm the robustness of our results, increase their validity, and strengthen the implications of our findings for theory and management.

From a conceptual perspective, we propose a new approach to co-production, such that we differentiate non-transferable (i.e., tasks that must be delivered by the customer) and transferable (i.e., tasks that can be delivered by the customer) forms. Distinguishing these two types of co-production improves understanding co-production itself and, by offering a common definition for further research, supports the development of a coherent body of knowledge.

From a methodological perspective, this study is one of the first to manipulate co-production by a real-world exercise in a service process (for an additional example see Troye and Supphellen, 2012). In two studies, participants actually "worked" before consuming a co-produced service, which provided a direct implementation of co-production in an experimental design. To test the robustness of our results, we apply three approaches across different service contexts: First, we used an incentivized economic laboratory experiment to implement co-production and control for external effects due to the absence of any frames. Second, we framed co-production in a scenario-based and a field experiment. Third, in two additional scenario experiments, we identified moderators of the relationship between co-production and WTP, which would not be effectively possible in the monetarily incentivized experiment.

From a managerial perspective, our study provides insights into the extent to which consumers will expect price discounts or pay price premiums for varying levels of co-production. These insights support managers in designing their pricing strategy and implementing appropriate pricing instruments (e.g., price differentiation, price discrimination, value-based pricing, price bundling) if customers co-produce. The findings will also help managers with decisions relating to how co-production processes should be designed and which market segments should be targeted in order to realize higher prices.

References

Auh S, Bell SJ, McLeod CS, Shih E (2007) Co-production and customer loyalty in financial services. Journal of Retailing 83(3):359–370, DOI 10.1016/j.jretai.2007.03.001

Bendapudi N, Leone RP (2003) Psychological implications of customer participation in co-production. Journal of Marketing 67(1):14–28

Bowen DE (1986) Managing customers as human resources in service organizations. Human Resource Management 25(3):371–383, DOI 10.1002/hrm.3930250304

Gallan A, Jarvis C, Brown S, Bitner M (2013) Customer positivity and participation in services: An empirical test in a health care context. Journal of the Academy of Marketing Science 41(3):338–356, DOI 10.1007/s11747-012-0307-4

Groth M (2005) Customers as good soldiers: Examining citizenship behaviors in internet service deliveries. Journal of Management 31(1):7–27, DOI 10.1177/0149206304271375

Guo L, Arnould EJ, Gruen TW, Tang C (2013) Socializing to co-produce: Pathways to consumers' financial well-being. Journal of Service Research DOI 10.1177/1094670513483904

Hill J (2011) Some supermarkets bagging self-checkout. (accessed July 14, 2013), URL http://www.cbsnews.com/2100-201_162-20111648.html

Kunz WH, Hogreve J (2011) Toward a deeper understanding of service marketing: The past, the present, and the future. International Journal of Research in Marketing 28(3):231–247

Lusch RF, Vargo SL, O'Brien M (2007) Competing through service: insights from service-dominant logic. Journal of Retailing 83(1):5–18

Mills PK, Hall JL, Leidecker JK, Margulies N (1983) Flexiform: A model for professional service organizations. The Academy of Management Review 8(1):118–131

Troye SV, Supphellen M (2012) Consumer participation in coproduction: "I made it myself" effects on consumers' sensory perceptions and evaluations of outcome and input product. Journal of Marketing 76:33–46

Wang T, Venkatesh R, Chatterjee R (2007) Reservation price as a range: An incentive-compatible measurement approach. Journal of Marketing Research 44(2):200–213

Yim CKB, Chan KW, Lam SS (2012) Do customers and employees enjoy service participation? Synergistic effects of self- and other-efficacy. Journal of Marketing 76(6):121–140

Mass Layoffs: When and How Do They Affect Customer Satisfaction?

Johannes Habel and Martin Klarmann

Downsizing seems to be one of the most appealing cost-cutting strategies to companies all around the world. Having emerged as a response to the economic slowdown of the 1980s (Baumol et al, 2003), this controversial management practice remains a topic of highest prominence even today. In fact, between 2000 and 2008 (i.e., even before the financial crisis) more than 10 million U.S. employees lost their jobs in over 52,000 mass layoff events (Bureau of Labor Statistics 2009).

Interestingly, previous research shows that the attempt to improve performance through mass layoffs often fails. In search for explanations, researchers have begun to examine the effects of mass layoffs (often referred to as "downsizing") on customer satisfaction and found first evidence of a negative relationship. As Chadwick et al (2004, p. 406) note, "The general consensus among researchers over the last two decades is that organizational performance is as likely to suffer as it is to improve after downsizing." In this context, marketing researchers have focused on understanding the effect of downsizing on customer satisfaction, with first studies reporting a negative relationship (Lewin, 2009; Lewin and Johnston, 2008; Lewin et al, 2010, e.g.).

Johannes Habel
Ruhr Universität Bochum

Martin Klarmann
Karlsruhe Institute of Technology
✉ martin.klarmann@kit.edu

CUSTOMER & SERVICE SYSTEMS
KIT SCIENTIFIC PUBLISHING
Vol. 1, No. 1, S. 55–58, 2014

DOI 10.5445/KSP/1000038784/07
ISSN 2198-8005
(cc) BY-SA

We argue that this issue may well be more complex. Drawing on a theoretical argument on the relationship between firm productivity and customer satisfaction by Anderson et al (1997), we propose that it will mostly depend on environmental factors whether downsizing has a positive or a negative effect on customer satisfaction. Consider for instance the customer involvement into the product category as a context factor. If customers are highly interested in a product category they are much more likely to notice

1. the downsizing itself and
2. resulting changes in product performance.

Hence, downsizing is much more likely to have a negative effect on customer satisfaction in this situation. Similarly, we expect that the negative effect of downsizing on customer satisfaction is stronger for service firms, organizations low on organizational slack and organizations where labor productivity is already high before the downsizing. Further, we expect a more pronounced effect on satisfaction if the mass layoffs are conducted proactively to further increase profits vs. reactively to help overcome an organizational crisis. Finally, due to possible effects of downsizing on innovative capabilities, we expect that the negative effect of downsizing on satisfaction is stronger in industries characterized by high R&D intensity.

To test our hypotheses, we combine data from three sources.

1. We use data from the American Customer Satisfaction Index (ACSI) to measure our focal variable customer satisfaction.
2. We measure organizational downsizing as well as most context factors using Compustat data.
3. To measure consumer industry involvement, we collected survey data.

The original sample for our study contains all companies listed in the ACSI. We excluded companies that either were not incorporated in the United States (e.g., BMW) or provided customer satisfaction data on the brand instead of the firm level (e.g., Chrysler Corporation, for which the ACSI differentiates between Chrysler and Dodge-Plymouth). We then matched these companies with financial data and employment information of Standard and Poor's Compustat, excluding companies that were not unequivocally listed on Compustat or did not provide three consecutive years of complete data. Also, we included data only up to the year 2008 in order to exclude any exceptional effects of the recent world economic crisis.

We used two measurement approaches for determining whether a firm had done downsizing or not.

1. Consistent with previous research we defined a dummy variable that indicated whether the total number of a firm's employees had gone down compared to the previous year by 5% or more. Based on this, we were able to identify more than 180 downsizing events.
2. We created a second narrower downsizing variable. Again this was a dummy variable, but to consider an employee reduction as downsizing it was additionally required that the mass layoff was also reported in a corresponding newspaper article in a major business journal.

Using various panel regression estimators on our data, we find a negative effect of downsizing on customer satisfaction. However, it is not statistically significant. As hypothesized we can report that the negative effect of downsizing on customer satisfaction is generally more pronounced if a company has low organizational slack, and if it operates in an R&D-intensive industry. Finally, as predicted, when using the broad downsizing operationalization there is a negative effect of downsizing in markets that customers feel highly involved with.

Our research makes at least three contributions to the discipline.

1. We identify situations in which the effect of downsizing on customer satisfaction is more pronounced.
2. By employing longitudinal data, our study allows us to make stronger causal claims regarding downsizing's effect on performance compared with previous research. This is particularly important, because a negative association between downsizing and customer satisfaction can also arise in cross-sectional data through an effect of customer satisfaction on downsizing. In fact it is quite plausible, that firms with unsatisfied customers will encounter performance problems that might entice them to engage in downsizing.
3. Our study also contributes to downsizing research by demonstrating how satisfaction outcomes of downsizing may explain whether a downsizing project is successful or not. By showing that downsizing may have an indirect effect on financial performance via customer satisfaction, our findings provide a possible explanation of why so

many downsizing projects fail. Thus, we also contribute to research on the so-called "hidden costs" of downsizing (Buono, 2003) by providing evidence that these hidden costs actually translate into monetary disadvantages.

The full paper is available on request from the authors.

References

Anderson EW, Fornell C, Rust RT (1997) Customer satisfaction, productivity, and profitability: Differences between goods and services. Marketing Science 16(2):129–145, DOI 10.1287/mksc.16.2.129

Baumol WJ, Blinder AS, Wolff EN (2003) Downsizing in America: Reality, Causes, and Consequences. Russell Sage Foundation, New York

Buono AF (2003) The hidden costs and benefits of organizational resizing activities. In: de Meuse KP, Marks ML (eds) Resizing the Organization: Managing Layoff, Divestitures, and Closings, Jossey-Bass, San Francisco, pp 306–346

Chadwick C, Hunter LW, Walston SL (2004) Effects of downsizing practices on the performance of hospitals. Strategic Management Journal 25(5):405–427, DOI 10.1002/smj.383

Lewin JE (2009) Business customers' satisfaction: What happens when suppliers downsize? Industrial Marketing Management 38(3):283–299, DOI 10.1016/j.indmarman.2007.11.005

Lewin JE, Johnston WJ (2008) The impact of supplier downsizing on performance, satisfaction over time, and repurchase intentions. Journal of Business & Industrial Marketing 23(4):249–255

Lewin JE, Biemans W, Ulaga W (2010) Firm downsizing and satisfaction among united states and european customers. Journal of Business Research 63(7):697–706, DOI 10.1016/j.jbusres.2009.05.005

Complaint Management and the Role of Relationship Quality

Lars Meyer-Waarden and William Sabadie

Abstract Facing dissatisfaction, customers have several alternatives: exit, loyalty and voice. The verbal answer (Voice) can be word-of-mouth communication or a complaint which is a constructive way to express dissatisfaction to obtain a correction or compensation. The management of complaints thus perfectly integrates within scope of customer relationship management to increase loyalty since it gives an organization a last chance to retain dissatisfied clients (Smith et al, 1999). In addition, complaints are a very rich source of valuable information to improve quality continuously. The investigations on complaint management show that the theory of justice (Adams, 1965) explains the satisfaction of complaining customers (Orsingher et al, 2010). However, the questions about the nature and the valence of the compensations as well as which consumer targets to privilege remain unanswered. The principal contribution of this article is thus to determine the most effective dimensions of the theory of justice in the context of customer complaint management to satisfy and retain customers. We differentiate the effectiveness of the complaint management process according to the relationship quality or strength between the firm and the customer. We first describe the key factors for complaint management and then we explain our conceptual model as well

Lars Meyer-Waarden
University Toulouse 1, CRM CNRS & EM Strasbourg, HuManiS
✉ meyerwaarden@em-strasbourg.eu

William Sabadie at
IAE Lyon, Magellan (EA 3713)
✉ william.sabadie@univ-lyon3.fr

CUSTOMER & SERVICE SYSTEMS
KIT SCIENTIFIC PUBLISHING
Vol. 1, No. 1, S. 59–68, 2014

DOI 10.5445/KSP/1000038784/08
ISSN 2198-8005
(cc) BY-SA

as our hypotheses and methodology. Finally, the article shows the results and finishes with a discussion, managerial implications and research directions.

1 Key factors in the management of complaints

The management of complaints aims at preserving the quality of a relationship. It is the one critical moment during which customers can test the reality of the recompensation efforts which the firm is ready to grant to satisfy them.

1.1 The role of relationship quality

The quality of the relationship indicates a psychological connection that customers have with a firm. It can be considered as a global judgment of the relationship (Garbarino and Johnson, 1999). In the literature a consensus is established about the importance of satisfaction, trust, commitment and identity connection which influence the quality of the relationship (Bhattacharya et al, 1995).

The role of relationship quality is complex in the complaint management process and service incidents (Grégoire and Fisher, 2006). On the one side, a strong relationship quality may have a protective effect (Ahluwalia, 2002; Bolton et al, 2000). A strong bond between a customer and a company (and thus strong loyalty) could result in lower expectations of the customer concerning the service quality (being less confronted to competitors' offers), a less severe judgment of the problem by the customer, and lead to more satisfaction with complaint management (Hess et al, 2003). Furthermore, a bad complaint management might have a less negatively influence on the customers' trust and commitment (Tax et al, 1998).

On the other hand, the relationship quality may lead to judgments and behaviors that are relatively more negative for the company. Indeed, customers with strong relationship quality may have higher expectations in terms of complaint management and might be particularily demanding, because they know that they are very good customers (Tax et al, 1998;

Kelley and Davis, 1994). They may be more inclined to feel betrayed, because the trust they had in the company has been disappointed by an incident of service (Wetzel et al, 2012).

1.2 The role of perceived justice

The theory of justice explains how individuals react to situations of conflicts. The perception of justice results from a three-dimensional evaluation (Smith et al, 1999; Tax et al, 1998). A meta-analysis (Orsingher et al, 2010) shows that distributive and interactional justice strongly influences the satisfaction and the behavior of complainers while procedural justice plays a very weak role. Thus, when consumers are dissatisfied and when they have a feeling of injustice, they make a complaint to restore the balance of the exchange from an economic and relational point of view. From an economic point of view, they wish to receive a proportional answer to their costs: the utility of the complaint must therefore be higher than the perceived costs, including those related to the treatment of the complaint (Grégoire et al, 2009). From a relational point of view, customers wish to be treated with consideration and respect by the company.

2 Hypotheses

The effectiveness of the complaint efforts of the company must be considered with regard to the type of customers (Bolton et al, 2000; Wetzel et al, 2012). The relationship quality with customers plays a fundamental moderating role on the compensations to be granted (Wetzel et al, 2012). If the relationship quality is good (bad), the level of necessary compensation efforts can (must) be lower (higher). A major weakness of this research is that these authors do not distinguish distributive and interactional efforts. We, therefore, suggest that the loyal individuals maintaining a strong relationship quality with the firm are searching more for interactional efforts than new customers. This could be justified by the importance of this dimension in the field of complaint management (Smith et al, 1999; Tax et al, 1998). In addition, the interactional efforts are more able to restore a contract of trust and the status of the customer who might feel betrayed because of the service incident. They would like to be recognized as such (Thibaut and Walker, 1975; Lind and Tyler, 1988):

H1   Loyal customers having a strong relationship quality with the firm prefer interactional (non-monetary) compensations to distributive (monetary) ones.
      On the other hand, new customers, having a low relationship quality with the firm, do not have identity connections with the company. They should therefore be attached to rebalance the exchange in economic terms:

H2   New customers having a weak relationship quality with the firm prefer distributive (monetary) compensations to interactional (non-monetary) ones.
      In this context, we distinguish two types of compensations: money refunding and purchase voucher. The purchase voucher symbolizes the desire of the firm and the customer to continue the relationship. That is why we suggest that the loyal customers having a strong relational quality with the firm are more willing to accept purchase vouchers than refunding. This is coherent with their complaints' targets to improve a given situation in case of dissatisfaction and to continue the relationship with the firm.

H3   Loyal customers having a strong relationship quality with the firm prefer purchase vouchers to money refunding.
      On the other hand, a new customer does not need to restore trust and inevitably has not committed yet into a new long term relationship.

H4   New customers having a weak relationship quality with the firm prefer refunding to purchase vouchers.
      Finally, the intensity of the effort of compensation (i.e. generosity) must be considered. In H1 we suggest that loyal customers having a strong relationship quality with the firm are more searching for consideration (interactional dimension) than economic benefits (distributive dimension). On the other hand, customers having a low relationship quality with the firm are more instrumentally orientated, and consequently, they are probably more sensitive to the intensity of the effort of compensation (i.e. the monetary value; (Smith et al, 1999)).

H5   The importance of the intensity of the effort of compensation is lower for loyal customers having a strong relationship quality with the firm than for new customers having a low relationship quality with the firm.

3 Methodology

To test our assumptions we choose the experimental methodology by scenario. The restaurant sector is selected, because consumption in a restaurant is a current situation and involves relatively frequent problems of non-quality, because of the importance and the complexity of the interpersonal relationships (i.e. customers and personnel in contact). Within the scenario the respondent invites his/her father at the restaurant for celebrating his 50th birthday. The incidents include long waiting in spite of reservation, poor dishes and quality, lack of reactivity of the staff.

We consider two types of distributive compensations to distinguish their relative impact and their valence and two interactional compensations:

1. The nature of compensation: The restaurant offers

   a. a purchase voucher to be used on a forthcoming consumption or
   b. money refunding.

2. The intensity (or the monetary value of refunding or the purchase voucher): The offer of the restaurant corresponds to

   a. the total amount (100%) or
   b. a part (66%) of the value of the meal.

3. The interactional compensation: We compare the situation where

   a. the owner contacts the complainer by telephone in order to apologize (i.e. strong relational value) or
   b. the restaurant sends an impersonalized email (i.e. low relational value).

8 compensation scenarios with $2 \times 2 \times 2$ dimensions (3 attributes of compensations having each 2 levels) were thus generated by an orthogonal design.

A pretest of the scenarios ($N = 80$) validates the experimental conditions:

1. In the case of strong relationship quality perceived trust (mean 5.95) and loyalty intention (mean 5.58) are significantly higher ($p < 0.01$), than in the case of low relationship quality (mean perceived trust 1.63 and mean loyalty intention 1.08).
2. The scenario incident is judged critical (mean 5.03) and the restaurant is judged responsible for the problem (mean 6.16).
3. Concerning justice, the response (personal apology with a mean of 3.93; "Apologizes of the staff were sincere") is perceived as more just than the impersonalized response (mean 2.78) with $p < 0.01$. The media of response (mail versus phone) does not influence the distributive justice ("the response gives me the impression to have good value for my money": $p > 0.2$).
4. But the intensity of compensation influences significantly the distributive justice (mean 100% compensation 4.02 vs. mean 66% compensation 3.13, $p < 0.01$), but does not influence interactional justice ($p > 0.5$).

The investigations have been carried out between 2010 and 2011 with 301 students from 3 French universities. The interviewees, either supposed to be a new client who comes for the first time ($N = 152$) or a loyal client having a strong relationship quality with the owner and a strong attachment to restaurant ($N = 149$), are invited to classify by descending preference the most desired compensation ("1") to the least preferred one ("8"). A random rotation of the scenarios is made before each investigation (type of client and scenario) to avoid systematic bias. To calculate the partial utilities of the attributes, a conjoint analysis is used.

4 Results

The relative importance of the compensations varies according to the type of client. Table 1 shows the importance of the attributes for new and loyal clients. Table 2 the partial utilities of the attributes' levels for new and loyal clients, respectively.

Table 1 Importance of attributes

Attribute	New Clients	Loyal Clients
Nature of Compensation	28%	8%
Intensity/Monetary Value	20%	9%
Interactional Compensation	52%	83%

Table 2 Partial utility (P.U.) of attribute levels

Attribute	Level	New Clients		Loyal Clients	
		P.U.	Std. Error	P. U.	Std. Error
Nature of	Voucher	-0.263	0.06	0.141	0.044
Compensation	Refund	0.263	0.06	-0,141	0.044
Intensity/	100%	0.182	0.06	0.147	0.044
Monetary Value	66%	-0.182	0.06	-0.147	0.044
Interactional	Personal call	1.211	0.06	1.401	0.044
Compensation	Impersonal mail	-1.211	0.06	-1.401	0.044
(Constant)		4.5	0.06	3.8	0.044

For loyal customers, compensations' interactional dimensions (i.e. the quality of the relationship) are much more important (83%) than for new customers (52%). H1 is thus validated. If the quality of the relationship with the firm is good, the compensations' distributive dimensions (nature of compensation (8%) and intensity of the effort (9%)) are significantly less important for loyal customers than for new customers. Moreover the purchase voucher, as expected in H3, is preferred to refunding by loyal customers. This confirms the intention of loyal customers to maintain the relationship with the supplier. In order to confirm this result, we carried out a supplementary inter-subject experiment with another group of students. For this, we created two scenarios:

1. the restaurant offers refunding ($N = 39$) or
2. a purchase voucher ($N = 31$).

In both cases, we only consider the case of loyal customers who are contacted by the owner of the restaurant who offers a compensation of a value equivalent to the amount of the meal. The feeling of perceived justice is not significantly different according to the nature of the compensation (mean of perceived justice for voucher (5.13) and for refunding (5.08), $p = 0.86$).

On the other hand, for new customers the nature (28%) and the value (20%) remain important, in spite of the fact that the relational value is the most important dimension. H2 is rejected, but it becomes clear that the relational component of the complaint is less important for new customers than loyal ones. Refunding as a compensation with less links to the supplier has higher partial utility (0.263) than purchase vouchers (−0.263). H4 is validated. Finally, in support with H5, the importance of the monetary value of the compensation is lower for loyal customers having a strong relationship quality with the firm. The differences are significant for all the assumptions (χ^2-test, $p < 0.01$ or 0.05).

5 Discussion and implications

The results show the importance of the relationship quality with the customer. On the one hand, the interactional efforts are preferred for all customers types (loyal vs. new). It is thus important to establish a direct relationship with the customers; a phone call is preferred to an email. The quality of the relationship thus influences the effectiveness of the complaint management. For loyal customers with strong relationship quality, the direct contact with the firm is by far the most important compensation element. It is important for them to re-establish a contract of trust and to be considered as "special clients". It might even enable firms to reduce the compensations' amounts. Lastly, loyal customers more easily accept purchase vouchers than refunding, because vouchers symbolize their intention to continue the relationship. These clients have more attachment to symbols than to money.

For new customers, even if interactional efforts constitute the most important factor, they try to rebalance the exchange in economic terms. They prefer re-funding, because they do not need to restore trust, and they do not necessarily try to establish a long term relationship in case of dissatisfaction. These clients have an instrumental orientation, and are more sensitive to the intensity of the effort of the compensation. It is thus very important that the firm grants them a compensation equal to the full value of the service.

For the management of complaints, it is important to understand which compensations are most valued according to the type of customers (new vs. loyal). This highlights the need for a differentiated reward management. The firm can offer limited distributive or monetary efforts to loyal customers, if managers pay attention to interactional or relational elements. On the other hand, the distributive efforts must be maximized, if the objective is to satisfy new customers.

Variables such as the sector, the responsibility of the company for the incident, and the customer involvement are likely to influence the results and could be integrated. On the theoretical level we study the impact of the compensations via preferences. It would be interesting to consider other variables of the complaint-handling process such as the perceived justice or satisfaction. The effectiveness of the complaint management could also be approached by the measure of purchase, word-of-mouth or retaliation intentions. The effects of interactions between the compensations could be studied more thoroughly. Finally, individual financial indicators, such as "Customer Lifetime Value", could be integrated in future research, to grant compensations according to the value of the customers. This last point is important as the profitability of a complaint management program must especially be measured by its profit contribution.

References

Adams J (1965) Inequity in social exchange. Advances in Experimental Social Psychology 2:267–299

Ahluwalia R (2002) How prevalent is the negativity effect in consumer environments? Journal of Consumer Research 29(3):270–79

Bhattacharya CB, Hayagreeva R, Glynn MA (1995) Understanding the bond of identification: An investigation of its correlates among art museum members. Journal of Marketing 59(4):46–57

Bolton R, Kannan P, Bramlett M (2000) Implications of loyalty program membership and service experiences for customer retention and value. Journal of the Academy of Marketing Science 28(1):95–108, DOI 10. 1177/0092070300281009

Garbarino E, Johnson MS (1999) A the different roles of satisfaction, trust, and commitment in customer relationships. Journal of Marketing 63(2):70–87

Grégoire Y, Fisher RJ (2006) The effects of relationship quality on customer retaliation. Marketing Letters 17(1):31–46

Grégoire Y, Tripp TR, Leroux M (2009) When customer love turns into lasting hate: The effects of relationship strength and time on customer revenge and avoidance. Journal of Marketing 73(4):18–32

Hess RL, Ganesan S, Klein NM (2003) Service failure and recovery: The impact of relationship factors on customer satisfaction. Journal of the Academy of Marketing Science 31(2):127–45

Kelley SW, Davis MA (1994) Antecedents to customer expectations to service recovery. Journal of the Academy of Marketing Science 22(3):52–61

Lind AE, Tyler TR (1988) The social psychology of procedural justice. Plenum, New York

Orsingher C, Valentini S, de Angelis M (2010) A meta-analysis of satisfaction with complaint handling in services. Journal of the Academy of Management Science 38:169–186

Smith AK, Bolton RN, Wagner J (1999) A model of customer satisfaction with service encounters involving failure and recovery. Journal of Marketing Research 36(3):356–372

Tax ST, Brown SW, Chandrashekaran M (1998) Customer evaluations of service complaint experiences: Implications for relationship marketing. Journal of Marketing 62:60–67

Thibaut J, Walker L (1975) Procedural Justice : A psychological analysis. Erlbaum, Hillsdale, NJ

Wetzel HA, Hammerschmidt M, Zablah AR (2012) Gratitude versus entitlement: An antagonistic process model of the profitability impact of customer prioritization. In: Proceedings of the 2012 Summer AMA Educators' Conference, Chicago, vol 23, pp 12–13

Customer-to-Customer Interactions within Online Review Sites: A Typology of Contributors

Andreas Munzel and Werner H. Kunz

Abstract As the Internet has become an increasingly relevant communication and exchange platform, social interactions exist online in multiple forms. Based on the literature on electronic word-of-mouth (eWOM) communication, social exchange theory and transformative consumer research, we conduct latent profile analysis to understand who engages in eWOM communication as well as how and why they do so. In addition to the traditional dichotomy of "posters" and "lurkers", we show that another group is included, which multiplies the scope of the WOM through transmission. By identifying and describing two active customer groups in addition to lurkers, our study provides insights into important user groups. Both groups are central for the service provider to manage the community and for understanding who contributes to social capital. Reciprocity as important mechanism in virtual environments presents a key condition for the development of social capital. Our research contributes to the growing field of consumer articulations online by empirically investigating why individuals engage online in social capital generation.

Andreas Munzel
EM Strasbourg Business School, HuManiS, University of Strasbourg, 61 Avenue de la Forêt Noire, 67085 Strasbourg, France,
✉ andreas.munzel@em-strasbourg.eu

Werner H. Kunz
College of Management, University of Massachusetts Boston, 100 Morrissey Boulevard, Boston, MA, 02125, United States,
✉ werner.kunz@umb.edu

CUSTOMER & SERVICE SYSTEMS   DOI 10.5445/KSP/1000038784/09
KIT SCIENTIFIC PUBLISHING   ISSN 2198-8005
Vol. 1, No. 1, S. 69–75, 2014

1 Introduction and research goals

Over the last years, electronic Word-of-Mouth (eWOM) has received considerable attention from academics. eWOM is referred to as "any positive or negative statement made by potential, actual, or former customers about a product or company, which is made available to a multitude of people and institutions via the Internet" (Hennig-Thurau et al, 2004). An increasing number of empirical studies have researched the effects of eWOM messages on purchasing intentions (Park and Lee, 2009), product and brand choice (Senecal and Nantel, 2004), consumer attitudes (Lee et al, 2008), and on sales (Chevalier and Mayzlin, 2006). Thus, there is numerous evidence that eWOM is beneficial for the company and offers them an effective marketing tool to compete in the marketplace.

However, eWOM is not only beneficial for companies, but also for the society at large. Sharing one's own experiences with other individuals online helps customers to connect with peers and builds social bonds (Belk and Llamas, 2011). These relational online interactions empower consumers to evaluate marketplace offerings and enable them to make better informed decisions (Kozinets, 1999). Thus, eWOM is a very effective consumption decision tool for individuals.

Whereas previous research has shown the relevance of eWOM for marketers and consumers (Huang et al, 2007), the literature lacks of empirical insights on the interdependence of individuals' eWOM behaviors in relation to their motives (Shao, 2009) and on the diversity of online interactions. This raises the following questions: Who are the individuals that are engaging in online activities and, therefore, in the generation of social capital for the public benefit? What are the applications that different user groups prefer? What drives them to serve the community on a regular basis?

To answer our research questions, we develop a framework based on the motivational psychology literature (Langens and Schmalt, 2008), social capital (Adler and Kwon, 2002) and social exchange theory (Blau, 1986). We followed a multi-step analysis approach – content analysis and latent profile analysis – to identify and differentiate groups of eWOM senders.

2 Method and results

We conducted an empirical study analyzing eWOM senders who posted hotel reviews on review sites (e.g., `TripAdvisor.com`). From a conceptual point of view, investigations of eWOM via online reviews are advantageous in that both first-order (e.g., writing a hotel review) and second-order eWOM (e.g., forwarding reviews and other content to friends) communication occur on these opinion platforms. We developed and programmed an online questionnaire and collaborated with a hotel review site, which posted the link transferring the participant to our online questionnaire at the end of the rating process. In total 693 site users participated in the study.

At the beginning of the questionnaire, we asked each respondent to explain in his own words the reason for writing the review. We used content analysis for analyzing the responses (Kassarjian, 1977). The results show that the written review was related to a positive experience for 48.5%, and to negative experiences for only 9.8% of the respondents. Nevertheless, the largest group of the consumers (i.e., 40.0%) was driven by altruistic motives without expressing any valence in their statements. The importance of giving something back to the community is also supported by the fact that 19.9% mentioned that they regularly read reviews and simultaneously expressed a desire to help other consumers.

In a second step, we used latent profile analysis to detect different underlying patterns of eWOM contributors. We used existing scales to measure the different activities and motives of the participants by using 7-point Likert scales ranging from 1 ("strongly disagree") to 7 ("strongly agree"). To classify the respondents with regard to their activities on the review site, we measured the degree of various possible activities. As recommended by the literature to reduce the set of variables for the latent profile analysis (Bacher et al, 2010), we reduced the various activities through factor analysis to 3 components: passive activities (e.g., reading reviews and ratings), active 2nd-order activities (e.g., forwarding others' reviews), and active 1st-order activities (e.g., writing reviews). We tested by means of the latent profile analysis a wide range of potential classification solutions and computed proportional class assignments based on the Bayes estimators. We decided to stick with the 3-class solution. Table 1 provides an overview of the identified classes.

Table 1 Overview of the 3 classes

	Overall		Class 1 Lurkers			Class 2 Creators			Class 3 Multipliers		
	n	%	n		%	n		%	n		%
Class size	693	(100)	382		(55.1)	94		(13.6)	217		(31.3)
Activities	$\bar{x}$	(ξ)	$\bar{x}_1$	$Sig.$	(ξ_1)	$\bar{x}_2$	$Sig.$	(ξ_2)	$\bar{x}_3$	$Sig.$	(ξ_3)
Passive	5.11	(1.29)	4.55	***	(1.27)	5.99	***	(0.76)	5.73	***	(1.00)
Active second-order	2.33	(1.36)	1.72	***	(0.76)	1.65	***	(0.61)	3.71	***	(1.41)
Active first-order	4.64	(1.69)	3.66	***	(1.44)	6.61	***	(0.48)	5.51	***	(1.12)
Booking hotels/travels	3.56	(2.12)	3.07	***	(1.97)	3.76		(2.32)	4.35	***	(2.04)
Motives	$\bar{x}$	(ξ)	$\bar{x}_1$	$Sig.$	(ξ_1)	$\bar{x}_2$	$Sig.$	(ξ_2)	$\bar{x}_3$	$Sig.$	(ξ_3)
Altruism based on positive experiences	5.61	(1.14)	5.19	***	(1.18)	6.21		(.73)	6.08	***	(0.90)
Altruism based on negative experiences	4.68	(1.59)	4.22	***	(1.54)	5.38	***	(1.44)	5.20	***	(1.46)
Venting negative feelings/ retaliation	1.86	(1.26)	1.71	***	(1.06)	2.15	*	(1.41)	2.01		(1.45)
Social bonding	2.39	(1.48)	2.06	**	(1.19)	2.10	***	(1.20)	3.10	***	(1.77)
Economic incentives	1.73	(1.26)	1.62	***	(1.09)	1.43	**	(0.86)	2.06	***	(1.57)
Intrinsic fun and enjoyment	2.76	(1.60)	2.38	***	(1.31)	3.01		(1.59)	3.31	***	(1.78)

Means and standard deviation in brackets.
$Sig.$: Significance of difference between overall mean and class mean.
$p < .1 : *; p < .05 : **; p < .01 : ***$.

Compared with the passive activities ($F = 108.13; p < .001; \eta^2 = .24$), the other two activities variables, active second-order activities ($F = 301.03; p < .001; \eta^2 = .47$) and active first-order activities ($F = 285.68; p < .001; \eta^2 = .45$), significantly contributed to the separation of the 3 classes. The first and largest class contains more than half of the participants in our sample. The members of this class - the lurkers - are more interested in passive activities ($M = 4.55; SD = 1.27$) than in the active 1st-order ($M = 3.66; SD = 1.44$) or active second-order activities ($M = 1.72; SD = .76$). The second class – the creators – represents the smallest class of the sample (13.6%). This class is primarily interested in the two core activities on the review site: reading ($M = 5.99; SD = .76$) and writing reviews ($M = 6.61; SD = .48$) and much less interested in second-order activities ($M = 1.65; SD = .61$). The third class contains almost one-third of the sample. The members in this class - labeled multipliers - are characterized by high means of their passive activities ($M = 5.73; SD = 1.00$)

and active first-order activities ($M = 5.51; SD = 1.12$). In addition, multipliers exhibit comparably greater interest in second-order activities ($M = 3.71; SD = 1.41$).

3 Discussion

The advent of the Internet has created a vast multitude of methods for sharing information, communicating with others, and expressing oneself. As stated by various scholars, prior research has largely ignored the specifics and potentially different manifestations of eWOM communication (Libai et al, 2010). To address this problem, we developed a framework that integrates first- and second-order eWOM. Based on this, we conducted a classification and motivational analysis of eWOM participants within the context of online hotel reviews. The results of the latent profile analysis reveal 3 classes of individuals, namely lurkers, creators and multipliers with regard to eWOM activities.

In our study, altruism-related motives clearly outranked the social bonding motive. This result can be linked to the characteristics of the environment in which we conducted our study - online review sites.

Furthermore, the notion of exchange and reciprocity appears to be increasingly important in the virtual field and should be further investigated in future research (Chan and Li, 2010). Individuals who are reading other people's opinions and experience reports may perceive a social debt and feel obliged to give something back to the community (Blau, 1986). Travelers can amortize this debt by contributing reviews in return.

Identifying and profiling contributors is an important issue for managers, particularly in the context of virtual communities (Wasko and Faraj, 2005; Sonnenbichler and Bazant, 2012). With regard to WOM research, practitioners show increasing interest in stimulating favorable customer-to-customer communication (Kumar et al, 2010).

References

Adler PS, Kwon SW (2002) Social capital: Prospects for a new concept. The Academy of Management Review 27(1):17–40

Bacher J, Pöge A, Wenzig K (2010) Clusteranalyse: Anwendungsorientierte Einführung in Klassifikationsverfahren, 3rd edn. Oldenbourg, München

Belk R, Llamas R (2011) The nature and effects of sharing in consumer behavior. In: Mick DG, Pettigrew S, Pechmann C, Ozanne JL (eds) Transformative Consumer Research for Personal and Collective Well-Being, Routledge, New York, pp 625–646

Blau PM (1986) Exchange and Power in Social Life, 2nd edn. Transaction, New Brunswick, NJ

Chan KW, Li SY (2010) Understanding consumer-to-consumer interactions in virtual communities: The salience of reciprocity. Journal of Business Research 63(9–10):1033–1040

Chevalier JA, Mayzlin D (2006) The effect of word of mouth on sales: Online book reviews. Journal of Marketing Research 43(3):345–354

Hennig-Thurau T, Gwinner KP, Walsh G, Gremler DD (2004) Electronic word-of-mouth via consumer-opinion platforms: What motivates consumers to articulate themselves on the internet? Journal of Interactive Marketing 18(1):38–52

Huang CY, Shen YZ, Lin HX, Chang SS (2007) Bloggers's motivations and behaviors: A model. Journal of Advertising Research 47(4):472–484

Kassarjian HH (1977) Content analysis in consumer research. The Journal of Consumer Research 4(1):8–18

Kozinets RV (1999) E-tribalized marketing?: The strategic implications of virtual communities of consumption. European Management Journal 17(3):252–264

Kumar V, Petersen JA, Leone RP (2010) Driving profitability by encouraging customer referrals: Who, when, and how. Journal of Marketing 74(5):1–17

Langens TA, Schmalt HD (2008) Motivational traits: New directions and measuring motives with the multi-motive grid (MMG). In: Boyle GJ, Matthews G, Saklofske DH (eds) The SAGE Handbook of Personality Theory and Assessment: Volume 1 – Personality Theories and Models, SAGE, London, pp 523–545

Lee J, Park DH, Han I (2008) The effect of negative online consumer reviews on product attitude: An information processing view. Electronic Commerce Research and Applications 7(3):341–352

Libai B, Bolton R, Bügel MS, De Ruyter K, Götz O, Risselada H, Stephen AT (2010) Customer-to-customer interactions: Broadening the scope of word of mouth research. Journal of Service Research 13(3):267–282

Park C, Lee TM (2009) Antecedents of online reviews' usage and purchase influence: An empirical comparison of U.S. and Korean consumers. Journal of Interactive Marketing 23(4):332–340

Senecal S, Nantel J (2004) The influence of online product recommendations on consumers' online choices. Journal of Retailing 80(2):159–169

Shao G (2009) Understanding the appeal of user-generated media: A uses and gratification perspective. Internet Research 19(1):7–25

Sonnenbichler A, Bazant C (2012) Application of a community membership life cycle model on tag-based communities in twitter. In: Gaul WA, Geyer-Schulz A, Schmidt-Thieme L, Kunze J (eds) Challenges at the Interface of Data Analysis, Computer Science, and Optimization, Studies in Classification, Data Analysis, and Knowledge Organization, Springer, Berlin/Heidelberg, pp 301–309, DOI 10.1007/978-3-642-24466-7_31

Wasko MM, Faraj S (2005) Why should i share? examining social capital and knowledge contribution in electronic networks of practice. MIS Quarterly 29(1):35–57

Converting Opinion Seekers in Opinion Givers in the Tourism Industry: Building Trust is Critical!

Gilles N'Goala and Caroline Morrongiello

Abstract With the Web 2.0, the interpersonal influence now includes its extension in cyberspace with electronic word of mouth. Thus, consumers become producers of information and create content. However, companies face difficulties in making them "partial employees" who will actively participate in co-creating value, in content production and in promoting their products on the web. From a literature review and a qualitative study, we identify eight possible antecedents of consumer participation and customer engagement towards a brand. Using structural equations modeling, we test our model in a French Ski Resort ($N = 1352$) and demonstrate that consumers actively participate in opinion platforms to help companies (resort, destination) and not to vent negative feelings. The low level of consumer participation in opinion platforms is mainly due to their high level skepticism regarding the sincerity of online reviews and the companies' opportunistic and manipulative practices (false reviews, etc.). Companies should trust their customers if they want them to become active promoters of their services on the internet.

Gilles N'Goala, Professor
Montpellier Research in Management (MRM), Université Montpellier 1, Avenue Raymond Dugrand CS 59640, 34960 Montpellier Cedex 2 - France,
✉ gilles.ngoala@univ-montp1.fr

Caroline Morrongiello, PhD Student
IREGE IAE Savoie Mont-Blanc, Université de Savoie, 4 Chemin de Bellevue, 74944 Annecy-le-Vieux,
✉ caroline.morrongiello@univ-savoie.fr

CUSTOMER & SERVICE SYSTEMS
KIT SCIENTIFIC PUBLISHING
Vol. 1, No. 1, S. 77–90, 2014

DOI 10.5445/KSP/1000038784/10
ISSN 2198-8005
(cc) BY-SA

1 Introduction

The development of Web 2.0 breaks the rules of many industries, and
especially of the tourism industry. Tourism providers (hotels, restaurants
etc..) do not even fully control their communication and have to face three
new phenomena:

1. the omnipresence of specialized community sites, and in particular
   Tripadvisor (40 million unique visitors / month, 40 million reviews,
   14 languages),
2. the rise of online travel agencies (oppodo, booking, expedia, etc.) that
   gather almost 3/4 of published comments today,
3. the emergence of new "voices" on travel blogs, travelers' forums and
   on social networks (Facebook, etc.).

Companies have then two contradictory objectives: On the one hand,
they aim at controlling and influencing what is said online, since they
do not really trust their customers and are afraid of the potential negative impact of negative word of mouth (WOM); on the other hand, they
want to have engaged customers, who articulate themselves on the Internet, express positive WOM and generate contents on their websites
(Van Doorn et al, 2010). However, they face many difficulties to engage
their customers to participate in content production on the web 2.0. From
our empirical study in France for instance, we found that 56% of consumers read the other tourists' online reviews before a journey, but only
28% actively participate and give their opinion after their journey. Companies then have to fight against the passivity of the silent majority of
customers who passively read online reviews (opinion seekers) but do not
actively participate (opinion givers) (Moe et al, 2011).

Empirical studies have been done to examine what generally motivates consumers to articulate themselves offline (Dichter, 1966; Engel
et al, 1993; Sundaram et al, 1998) and online (Hennig-Thurau et al, 2004;
Moe and Trusov, 2011). While the literature looks at what motivates consumers to post online reviews in general, our study aims at understanding what is the impact of individual factors (such as self-confidence) about
a specific brand (a ski resort) with the backdrop of the consumer/brand
relationship (brand attachment). Furthermore, prior research underesti-
mates the potential impact of consumers' skepticism about opinion platforms, which is growing, because companies manage their e-reputation

and are suspected to manipulate online reviews. Given that companies aim at controlling and managing their e-reputation on opinion platforms, consumers might be more reluctant to post comments and evaluations and to be actively engaged towards brands. The purpose of this paper is therefore to better understand why and how tourists participate in the web 2.0 and decide to post online reviews on different opinion platforms, such as specialized community websites, online travel agencies' websites, hotels and restaurants' websites, blogs, travelers' forums and social networks. While previous studies highlight general motives for eWOM (altruism, revenge, etc.), we hereafter also consider the individual factor of self-confidence, consumer skepticism about opinion platforms and consumer attachment to the brand.

Firstly, we present a brief literature review on consumer participation in the web 2.0 and on customer engagement to highlight the potential antecedents which have already been emphasized in prior research. Secondly, we present the results of a qualitative study that aimed at deeply understanding the way tourists act and react to opinion platforms. This allows us to highlight additional antecedents to eWOM. From the literature review and the preliminary qualitative study, we then elaborate a conceptual framework and develop hypotheses. Afterward, we show the results of a quantitative study conducted among tourists of a French Ski Resort (Le Grand Bornand, N=1352). Finally, we will draw conclusions from our studies and discuss theoretical and managerial implications.

2 Literature review: Antecedents of customer engagement

For Keller and Berry (2006), 90% of word of mouth conversations take place offline, and these "conversation catalysts" now rely heavily on the Internet as a resource to convey this information to their families and friends. This marketing communication model is more horizontal and customer engagement behavior (CEB) is a key objective. Van Doorn et al (2010) defined CEB, beyond brand communities, as *"the customer's behavioral manifestation toward a brand or firm, beyond purchase, resulting from motivational drivers. CEBs include a vast array of behaviors including word-of-mouth (WOM) activity, recommendations, helping other customers, blogging, writing reviews, and even engaging in legal action"*. Web

2.0 could be both an opportunity (interactivity and value co-creation) and a threat (loss of control over reputation). According to Moe et al (2011), customers always seek the opinions of others before making a purchase and it is much less common for customers to share their opinions online.

They show that the opinions that potential buyers and social media strategists read only come from a small segment of consumers. But the objective of web 2.0 is not just to identify a relative small number of influential, knowledgeable, communicable and innovative opinion leaders having an influence on a large number of followers. The electronic word of mouth relies heavily on thousands of customers having a personal experience with specific products and services. Therefore, we need to determine what could lead the majority of customers to break the silence. Most empirical studies (see Table 1) do not relate opinion seeking and opinion giving, whereas opinion giving may also depend on consumers' opinions and skepticism concerning opinion platforms.

While the literature looks at what motivates consumers to post online reviews in general (Hennig-Thurau et al, 2004), we still miss empirical studies which consider the potential impact of individual factors (such as self-confidence) about a specific brand (Le Grand-Bornand resort) with the backdrop of the consumer/brand relationship. We aim at filling this gap.

3 Qualitative Study

During a first stage, a qualitative study was conducted with the intention to understand why people seek and share personal opinions on the Internet and the way they do it. It was conducted at Le Grand Bornand, a French-Alps ski resort. The semi-directive interviews were conducted as individual interviews with 16 tourists. Each interview lasted 45 minutes. The first part of the interview guide that we developed dealt with the experience of tourists to the station. Respondents were then placed in front of a computer and they had to post a comment about their stay and then, they had to consult comments on the web and react. This allowed us to put them in the position of opinion-platforms users and bring out a number of themes that are omnipresent in the discourse of Internet users. To analyze the content, a thematic analysis was conducted by

Table 1 WOM and eWOM antecedents

AUTHORS	Dichter (1966)	Engel et al (1993)	Sundaram et al (1998)	Hennig-Thurau et al (2004)
CONCEPTS	Word-of-Mouth (WOM)			Electronic Word-of-Mouth (eWOM)
CONCEPT DEFINITION	WOM is an informal mode of communication between private parties concerning the evaluation of goods and services	WOM is an interpersonal influence where information is sought as well as given.	WOM is a form of interpersonal communication among consumers concerning their personal experiences with a firm or a product. It can be positive or negative (NWOM). The NWOM is correlated with negative consumption experiences.	eWOM is any positive or negative statement made by potential, actual, or former customers about a product or company, which is made available to a multitude of people and institutions via the Internet
IDENTIFIED ANTECEDENTS	Product involvement	Involvement	Product involvement; vengeance; anxiety reduction	Venting negative feelings
	Self involvement	Self enhancement	Self enhancement	Enhance their own self work; positive self enhancement
	Other involvement	Concern for others	Altruism; helping the company	Concern for other; helping the company
	Message involvement	Message intrigue		
		Cognitive dissonance		

grouping by themes the respondents' observations (Savoie-Zajc, 2000). We then carried out the coding operations of the observations. The aim during this content analysis phase consisted of applying to the corpus data processing that allows the access to a different meaning without distorting the original content. Therefore, we have categorized the topics putting together common elements under the following headings: exerting power and setting freedom of expression, rewards and punishments given to professionals, self-confidence in the ski resort choice, skepticism concerning the potential influence on others, difficulty in forming an opinion based on very different evaluations, distrust toward the professionals' practices on the web (hotels, restaurants, etc.), and attachment to the resort.

This research confirms and complements previous studies (Hennig-Thurau et al, 2004) which underline general personal motivations, but fail to consider individual factors (self-confidence) and consumers' skepticism about opinion platforms. We also note that consumers do not seek the approval of others and ego-reinforcement through web 2.0 participation. In most opinion platforms, most comments and evaluations are totally anonymous (except for social networks). In this qualitative study, we simultaneously consider opinion seeking and opinion giving and show that these activities are not totally independent. Moreover, in the tourism industry, we note that consumers' identification and affiliation with the resort strongly influences their participation in opinion platforms: The more committed to the service brand the consumers are, the more active they are likely to be on opinion platforms.

4 Conceptual framework and hypotheses

Based on prior literature and qualitative study, we elaborate a conceptual framework to explain consumer participation in opinion platforms in general as well as customer engagement behavior regarding a specific brand in particular (see Fig. 1). Firstly, we highlight personal motives, which lead consumers to articulate themselves on opinion platforms. Previous studies (Hennig-Thurau et al, 2004) underline that consumers express their opinions to:

1. help other consumers (altruism), without expecting any rewards in return,
2. exert power, e.g. influence companies' decisions and restore equity in consumer-company relationships,
3. venting negative feelings (vengeance) and attribute rewards and punishments to companies,
4. helping the company, in improving its services and developing its activities.

We also assume the potential role of three types of consumer confidence:

1. confidence in themselves in their skills and ability to select a good product/service (self-confidence is a dimension of personality that reflects a person's perceived control over him or herself and the environment, which is based on a personal history of successful goal-directed behavior, Tafarodi and Swann (1996)),
2. confidence in others' comments and evaluations, in particular in the sincerity of the opinions delivered online,
3. confidence in the marketers' online practices.

Previous studies (Sher and Lee, 2009) underline that online reviews foster consumer skepticism and cast doubts on trustworthiness of these online messages. The authors see consumer skepticism as a consumer tendency to believe or disbelieve in online reviews. In our study, we postulate that skepticism is not a consumer individual variable but a situational variable based on online reviews' perceived sincerity. When consumers are suspicious about the companies' practices on opinion platforms (false comments, e-reputation management, etc.), they are less likely to participate. In contrast, when they believe in the sincerity of other consumers' comments and evaluations found on these platforms, they are more likely to share and express their opinions with them by reciprocity. The source credibility remains a key driver of communication. Furthermore, self-confident consumers are less reluctant to share their opinions, since they believe they have an expertise in the field (tourism, ski resort, etc.) which could be useful for others. We also integrate an additional antecedent to consumer participation on opinion platforms concerning a specific brand: consumers' attachment to the brand. Park et al (2010) define *"brand attachment as the strength of the bond connecting the brand with the self"*. Since the brand represents who they are (e.g. an identity basis) or because it is personally relevant (an instrumentality basis), consumers are more likely to actively promote its products and services online and to become its "advocates" in opinion platforms. Therefore, we develop our hypotheses by drawing upon the theoretical frameworks on the motives of WOM and eWOM that we discuss above (Tabular 1). Our main hypotheses are summarized in Figure 1.

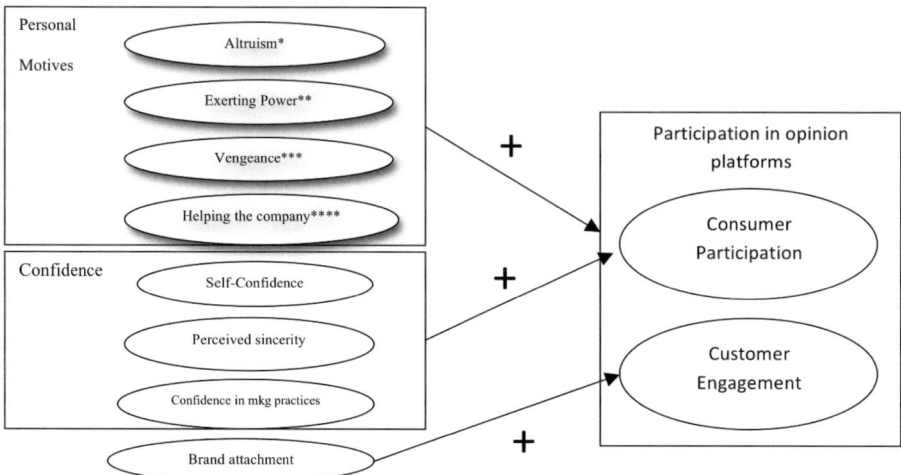

Fig. 1 A conceptual framework of the study

5 Quantitative Study

During a second stage, a quantitative study was conducted with the intention to measure the impact of the previously identified variables on Internet-users information seeking and participation on the web 2.0. We sent a message to an emailing list provided by the Grand Bornand Tourist Office (Savoy). The survey was self-administered by the Internet using software sphinx online, we collected 1385 answers from Le Grand-Bornand tourists. To estimate general consumer participation, we asked them whether they have posted reviews, gradings or evaluations (yes / no) on six types of opinion platforms: Specialized community websites (trip advisor for instance), online travel agencies websites (expedia, etc.), hotels and restaurants' websites, blogs, travelers' forums and social networks (facebook for instance). Then, we summed up the scores to capture the level of consumers' participation in web 2.0 platforms (from 0 to 6). To apprehend customer engagement toward the Grand Bornand, we asked them to indicate how frequently they have posted online reviews concerning this ski resort during the last year (from 1 "never" to 5 "very often").

To measure the eight independent variables shown in Figure 1, we refer to measurement scales which have been developed in the literature (see Table 2). These measurement scales were then adapted to the e-

Table 2 Questionnaire

First part: "You and the tourism"	We asked questions about the frequency of holidays, ways of booking, behavior in case of satisfaction and dissatisfaction and trip preparation.
Second part: "You and the Internet"	We asked questions about Internet and opinion platforms uses. We used our qualitative results to workout items about exerting power, desire for vengeance, altruism toward company and toward other consumers, skepticism toward professionals' practices, willingness to help companies (resorts)
Third part: "You and Le Grand-Bornand"	We asked questions about frequency, pattern, location and behavior on the web regarding Le Grand Bornand. We also measure the psychological attachment between the individual and the ski resort (Lacoeuilhe: brand attachment scale, 1999)

tourism context and translated into French. We used the same format for all items - Likert scales ranging from 1 (strongly disagree) to 5 (strongly agree) - in order to make answering easier and increase the response rate. As suggested by Churchill (1979), we implemented an iterative process to improve the measurement scales' reliability and validity. The questionnaire was first administered to master's students and then, after measurement scale purification, to the final sample. Our constructs were then refined in order to improve the psychometric qualities of our measurement scales. We first performed an exploratory factor analysis (oblimin). As expected, this led to the extraction of ten factors. The measurement scales show the psychometric qualities (reliability and validity) to be adequate, even though the items were mixed in the questionnaire so as to not artificially increase the validity of the measures. Then, using the structural equations method (AMOS software), we performed a Confirmatory Factor Analysis with these 8 constructs (latent variables) and 32 items (manifest variables). We observe that all constructs exhibit a satisfactory degree of convergent validity: standardized factor loadings are all significant and vary between 0.60 and 0.94; the average variances extracted vary between 0.50 and 0.78, which means the variance of each construct is better explained by its measures than by error (Fornell and Larcker, 1981). Reliability coefficients (Rho) are also satisfactory (between 0.80 and 0.91).

Table 3 Results

Antecedents	Consequences	Standardized Coefficient	P
	Consumer participation		
Altruism		-0.00	0.99
Exerting power		-0.05	0.55
Vengeance		0.02	0.75
Help the company		0.36	0.00
Self-confidence		-0.07	0.06
Perceived sincerity of online reviews		0.22	0.00
Confidence in marketing practices		-0.07	0.04
	Customer engagement		
Altruism		0.07	0.33
Exerting power		-0.12	0.12
Vengeance		0.04	0.63
Help the company		0.32	0.00
Self-confidence		0.01	0.74
Perceived sincerity of online reviews		0.15	0.00
Confidence in marketing practices		-0.03	0.47
Brand Attachment		0.19	0.00

6 Main results

From our total sample (N=1382), we found that 753 (56%) are opinion seekers and have read or posted online reviews during the last five years. While 56% read online reviews on tourism, half of them (28%) are opinion givers and have already posted comments, reviews, evaluations, etc. on - at least - one of the web 2.0 platforms (specialized community websites, online travel agencies websites, blogs, travelers' forums or social networks). Since we address the issue of converting these opinion seekers in opinion givers, we hereafter focus on these 753 consumers and do not consider other tourists who have no experience with opinion platforms. We apply structural equation modeling (Amos software) to test our hypotheses presented in Figure 1 (RMSEA=0.06). Results are shown in Table 3.

Our main findings are: Firstly, consumers tend to post online reviews to help the companies in improving their services and promoting their destination. It has an effect on general consumer participation (β=0.36, P <0.01) and also on customer engagement towards the Grand Bornand ski resort (β=0.32, P<0.01). Secondly, the perceived sincerity of posted reviews is critical to consumers' general participation (β=0.22, P<0.01) and engagement (β=0.15, P<0.01). To convert opinion seekers in opinion givers, managers have to build consumer confidence in opinion platforms. Thirdly, as expected in Figure 1, brand attachment has also a positive influence on customer engagement on opinion platforms (β=0.19, P<0.01). Fourthly, contrary to our expectations, we found that consumer skepticism concerning online marketing practices tends to enhance their participation in opinion platforms. In other words, consumers aim at fighting against marketers' manipulative practices by sharing their own experiences with other consumers. The more skeptical they are, the more active they will be. Fifthly, contrary to prior literature on WOM and e-WOM, altruism, exerting power or desire of vengeance are not drivers of consumer participation on opinion platforms dedicated to tourism. These personal motives do not have any impact. Finally, self-confidence has no significant influence on consumer participation and customer engagement. However, we note that self-confidence has a negative effect on consumer participation at the p< 0.10 level (β=-0.07, P<0.10). This raises additional questions, since, contrary to our expectations, the more self-confident tourists are, the less active they are on opinion platforms. Given their subjective expertise, they may believe they do not need any information from other customers.

7 Discussion

The purpose of our study was to explore the effects of personal motives, confidence and brand attachment on consumer participation on opinion platforms dedicated to tourism, and the mechanism supporting the effects. A qualitative and a quantitative study were conducted. Two majors findings emerged: first, the perceived sincerity of online reviews has a major role in consumer participation and second, the desire to help the company influences consumer participation and customer engagement towards the ski resort. Our empirical study (N = 1352) also leads to results which contradict prior literature on WOM and e-WOM. These findings contribute to a better understanding of the mechanism of online consumer participation and customer engagement antecedents. Most tourists want to help companies (resort, destination) and do not see their participation in opinion platforms as destructive acts (vengeance). Managers in tourism should therefore communicate on the sincerity of online reviews and avoid opportunistic online practices. They can trust their customers and let the "invisible hand" regulate the consumers' opinions. Otherwise, they will not be able to convert their customers in opinions givers, content generators and promoters of their destination.

Further investigation is needed concerning the possible opposite effects of skepticism on customer participation (Boush et al, 1994; Forehand and Grier, 2003): some consumers who are skeptical towards opinion platforms might be reluctant to make efforts and write comments, considering their lack of power or influence. In contrast, as we show, some consumers who are skeptical towards opinion platforms might also increase their participation in online opinion platforms to "tell the truth", contribute to more transparency and authenticity, and regulate the markets. Depending on the customer (age, gender, personal innovativeness, etc.), skepticism might lead to activity or inactivity. To uncover the mechanisms that block users from writing online reviews, personal barriers such as fear, ego, shyness, etc. might also be investigated. Companies could make use of these differences and differentiate their strategies.

Acknowledgements This research has been presented at the 42nd EMAC conference, Istanbul, June 4-7, 2013.

References

Boush DM, Friestad M, Rose GM (1994) Adolescent skepticism toward tv advertising and knowledge of advertiser tactics. The Journal of Consumer Research 21:165–175

Churchill GA (1979) A paradigm for developing better measures of marketing constructs. Journal of Marketing Research 16(1):64–73

Dichter E (1966) How word-of-mouth advertising works. Harvard Business Review 44:147–166

Engel JF, Blackwell RD, Miniard PW (1993) Consumer Behavior, 8th edn. Dryden Press, Fort Worth

Forehand MR, Grier S (2003) When is honesty the best policy? the effect of stated intent on consumer skepticism. Journal of Consumer Psychology 13(3):349–356

Fornell C, Larcker DF (1981) Structural equation models with unobservable variables and measurement error: Algebra and statistics. Journal of Marketing Research 18:382–388

Hennig-Thurau T, Walsh G (2003) Electronic word-of-mouth: Consequences of and motives for reading customer articulations on the Internet. International Journal of Electronic Commerce 8(2):51–74

Hennig-Thurau T, Gwinner KP, Walsh G, Gremle DD (2004) Electronic word-of-mouth via consumer-opinion platforms: What motivates consumers to articulate themselves on the internet? Journal of Interactive Marketing 18(1):38–52

Keller E, Berry J (2006) Word-of-mouth: The real action is offline. Advertising Age 77(20)

Lacoeuilhe J (1999) Proposition d'une échelle de mesure de l'attachement ã la marque. In: Congrès de l'Association Française du Marketing, pp 1067–1085

Marlowe D, Crowne DP (1960) A new scale of social desirability independent of psychopathology. Journal of Consulting Psychology 24(4):349–354

Moe WW, Trusov M (2011) The value of social dynamics in online product ratings forums. Journal of Marketing Research 48(3):444–456

Moe WW, Schweidel DA, Trusov M (2011) What influences customers' online comments. MIT Sloan Management Review

Park CW, MacInnis DJ, Priester J, Eisingerich AB, Iacobucci D (2010) Brand attachment and brand attitude strength: Conceptual and empirical differentiation of two critical brand equity drivers. Journal of Marketing 74(6):1–17

Porter LW, Steers RM, Mowday RT, Boultian PV (1974) Organizational commitment, job satisfaction, and turnover among psychiatric technicians. Journal of Applied Psychology 59:603–609

Savoie-Zajc L (2000) L'analyse des données qualitatives: Pratiques traditionnelle et assistée par le logiciel NUD*IST. Recherches qualitatives 21:99–123

Sher P, Lee S (2009) Consumer skepticism and online reviews: An elaboration likelihood model perspective. social behavior and personality. Journal of Applied Psychology 37(1):137–143

Sundaram DS, Mitra K, Webster C (1998) Word-of-mouth communications: A motivational analysis. Advances in Consumer Research 25:527–531

Tafarodi RW, Swann WB Jr (1996) Individualism-collectivism and global
    self-esteem: Evidence for a cultural trade-off. Journal of Cross-Cultural
    Psychology 27(6):651–672
Van Doorn J, Lemon K, Mittal V, Naß S, Pick D, Pirner P, Verhoef P (2010)
    Customer engagement behavior: Theoretical foundations and research
    directions. Journal of Service Research 13(3):253–266

How Web 2.0 Tools Impact The Museum-Visitor Relationship

Jessie Pallud

Abstract Cultural institutions such as museums increasingly rely on social media to achieve their missions. However, little attention has been paid to museums' strategies of communication with social media. Even if some research has focused more on visitor experience, there has been neither a particular stress on visitors' experience with social media nor on an evaluation of museums' strategies with these tools. Therefore, the objective of this paper is to explore how museums use social media to enhance their relationship with visitors and to determine if visitor empowerment is real. Since information systems (IS) research has paid scant attention to the role played by social media in museums' strategies, our work in-progress can help to fill this gap. This study has practical implications as well, because we try to identify how social media can help museums to be more competitive.

1 Introduction

According to a recent report on social media adoption, 86% of online US adults and 79% of European online adults engage with social media (Elliott and Sverdlov, 2012). Indeed, an increasing number of people across the world engage actively with online activities. Social media can be de-

Jessie Pallud
Ecole de Management Strasbourg, HuManiS
✉ jessie.pallud@em-strasbourg.eu

CUSTOMER & SERVICE SYSTEMS
KIT SCIENTIFIC PUBLISHING
Vol. 1, No. 1, S. 91–101, 2014

DOI 10.5445/KSP/1000038784/11
ISSN 2198-8005
(cc) BY-SA

fined as "a group of Internet-based applications that build on the ideological and technological foundations of Web 2.0, and that allow the creation and exchange of user generated content" (Kaplan and Haenlein, 2010, p. 61). Social technologies have emerged with the Web 2.0 paradigm which puts the emphasis on participation, sharing, accessibility, and user empowerment. These characteristics of the new Web have transformed companies' relationships with their customers (Bernoff and Li, 2008; Foster et al, 2010; Kaplan and Haenlein, 2010). The phenomenon of participation is not limited to the business context only, since cultural institutions such as museums increasingly rely on these social media to achieve their missions.

As a matter of fact, most of the well-known museums, such as The Louvre, the Museum of Modern Art (MOMA), the Guggenheim Museum, the Victoria and Albert Museum have online presences on Facebook and Twitter. During the first quarter of 2012, the MOMA located in New York has reached one million fans on Facebook demonstrating the potential of these tools to create huge communities of visitors and to expand knowledge beyond the museum wall. Among the fifty most active museums on social media, The Tate Museum was ranked second in February 2012 with 547,102 followers on Twitter (Lochon, 2012). While Russo et al (2008) contented that museums were slow to adopt social media technologies, we now observe higher enthusiasm and a multiplication of museums' initiatives with social media. In 2010, 43% of the French museums reported having a Facebook account, 18% a Twitter and Youtube account and 31% a Dailymotion account (Groupe EAC, 2011).

Cultural heritage institutions, like museums, are worthy of being studied because they contribute to social and economic developments of countries (Dümcke and Gnedovsky, 2013). France, which is the number one cultural tourism destination in Europe, lists 1200 national museums attracting more than 70 million visitors per year (France Diplomatie, 2006). Consequently, museums can also contribute to the economic growth of countries. This occurs not only in Europe, but, according to the Association of American Museums (AAM), they are "drivers of economy" in many places in the world.

However, little attention has been paid to museums' strategies of communication with social media. Even if some research has focused more on visitor experience, there has been neither a particular stress on visitors' experience with social media nor on an evaluation of strategies of museums with these tools. Therefore, the objective of this paper is to explore how museums use social media to enhance their relationship with visitors and visitors' participation with these media. Our research questions are the following:

- To what extent do social media help museums to meet visitors' expectation?
- Do visitors have a voice with these technologies?

In order to answer these research questions, we will review the literature on museum strategies with social media.

Since research has paid scant attention to the role played by social media in strategies of museum, our study can help to fill in this gap. This study has practical implications as well because we try to identify how social media can help museums to be more competitive. "A museum must be accountable for the economic use of resources at its disposal in an efficient manner and meet the standards for public trust and accountability" (Zorloni, 2012, p. 43). Therefore, museums can no longer be elitist institutions and must now try to attract the largest possible client base. Social media represent a potential solution to connect with visitors and to attract new publics. However, we want to determine if visitor empowerment is real.

This paper is structured as follows. First, we define and present the missions of a museum. Second, the context of the research is set out by analysing the relationship that exists between museums and their visitors. Third, we review the literature on social media and strategies of museums. Fourth, we conclude this research by introducing the methodology that may be employed in future research.

2 Definition and Missions of a Museum

Several practical definitions of museums are available. The one that is the most recognized and used widely in the museum field is that of the International Council of Museums (ICOM). According to the statutes of ICOM, "A museum is a non-profit making, permanent institution in the service of society and of its development, and open to the public, which acquires, conserves, researches, communicates and exhibits, for purposes of study, education and enjoyment, material evidence of people and their environment." (2001, Article 2). Consequently, museums are different from firms. Indeed, a museum is a non-profit making institution so even if it might contribute to a country's economic growth by attracting tourists, its existential goal is not profit (Bloch, 2004). Furthermore, museums have four principal missions. They are: (1) acquisition, (2) research, (3) communication and (4) exhibition. Porter (2006) described the museum value chain and he suggests a slightly different classification of these main missions. The primary activities of a museum are: (1) collection, (2) exhibition and programs, (3) visitor services and (4) marketing and sales.

Šola and Museoliitto (1997) also contend that museums and their visitors have a mutually beneficial relationship. Consequently, museums should try to develop ties with their visitors and this implies a two-way relationship. Museums communicate and exhibit their artefacts to the public. Conversely visitors should be able to communicate and share their thoughts with museums.

3 The Relationship of Museums with Their Visitors

The aforementioned characteristics of museums lead to the conclusion that there is a two-way relationship between visitors and museums, which supports the "mutual relationship" concept articulated by Šola and Museoliitto (1997). The contour of this relationship between museums and their visitors is elucidated below.

For a long time, a museology based on artefacts was dominant. In other words the objects were supposed to speak for themselves (Gob and Drouguet, 2003). More and more frequently, curators have become conscious that just displaying objects is not enough and that they need to give them meaning. Therefore, in addition to collection and documentation of artefacts, curators also have a mission of communication. They provide information in order to make objects more accessible (Gob and Drouguet, 2003).

Today, museum experts increasingly acknowledge that visitor interpretation plays an important role in their experience. Curators have become "visitor-centred" (Ross, 2004, p. 86) by putting more emphasis on visitor interpretation than on artefacts.

Furthermore, visitors are increasingly taking an active role within museums (Cameron, 2005). They try to give meaning to objects and not just take curators' interpretations for granted. Indeed, museum visits are more and more often perceived as an opportunity for individuals "to explore and make up their own minds, to test their own interpretations against the experts" (Hooper-Greenhill, 2000, p. 30). Visitors want to be able to develop their own thinking about phenomena or objects.

Museums have been for a long time influential institutions, since they were the only ones to convey meaning. The communication in this tradition was one way and visitors did not really have the chance to express themselves (Hicks 2005; Ross 2004). But today, power between curators and visitors is better balanced, especially through the usage of social media (Russo, 2011; Russo et al, 2008).

Social media introduce a new dimension, as they give "an enhancement of the traditional one-to-many information transfer model with a more genuinely interactive many-to-many communication model" (Russo et al, 2008). The traditional communication of museums with their visitors used to be one way and even when using technologies to communicate, curators focused on the diffusion of scientific content in a unilateral way. The recent development of social media enables visitors to react to this scientific content. Visitors can now communicate their thoughts or emotions directly to museum professionals or they can also discuss with other visitors (see Figure 1).

4 Social Media Strategies for Museums: Literature Review

What is clear is that even if museum attendance is growing, museums still struggle to accomplish their four core missions of collection, exhibition, education, and communication (Burton and Scott, 2003; Hooper-Greenhill, 2000; Russo, 2011). These challenges are partly due to new financial constraints. As a matter of fact, museums that used to be mainly public institutions tend either to become private or to see their governmental funding reduced (Russo, 2011). Furthermore, like companies museums also try to reach competitive advantage (Porter, 2006). Actually, museums are in competition with leisure and entertainment activities such as theatres, cinemas and concerts (Zorloni, 2012). Consequently, mu-

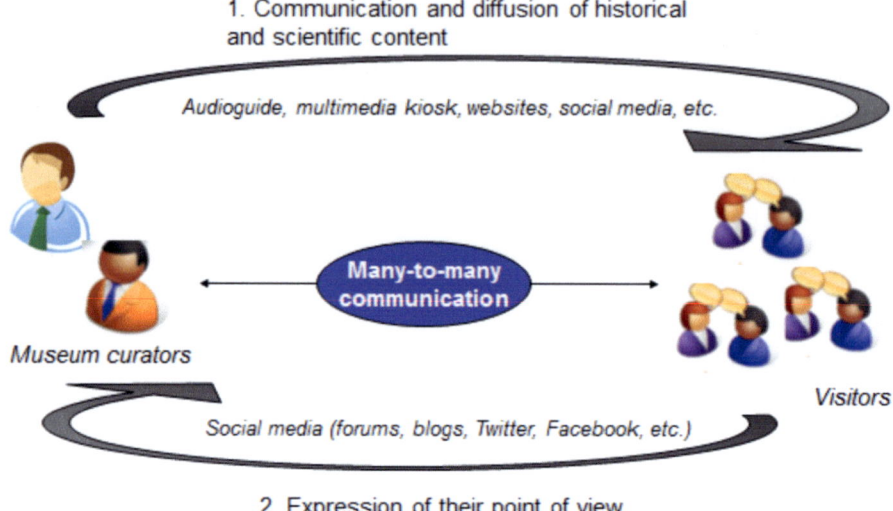

1. Communication and diffusion of historical and scientific content

Audioguide, multimedia kiosk, websites, social media, etc.

Many-to-many communication

Museum curators

Visitors

Social media (forums, blogs, Twitter, Facebook, etc.)

2. Expression of their point of view

Fig. 1 The Museum-Visitor Relationship

seums need to raise money and manage their activities more efficiently through organizational excellence. The performance of museums seems to be related to four perspectives: governance and finance perspective, public perspective, learning and growth perspective and intellectual perspective (Zorloni, 2012). Social media have the potential to contribute to each of these four perspectives.

For instance, social media could be used by museum professionals to create new forms of knowledge and innovation (Russo, 2011; Russo et al, 2008). By enabling visitors to contribute to cultural discussions, museums can enrich their intellectual perspective. Social media also impact the learning and growth perspective as they democratize access to cultural content (Proctor 2010). Table 1 summarizes some recent research on the role of social media in museums.

As presented in Table 1, prior research tends to focus on a specific facet of social media, namely the communication between museums and their visitors. This perspective is very important and is defined by Gallaugher and Ransbotham (2010) as the Magnet and Megaphone communication. More precisely, Gallaugher and Ransbotham (2010) argue that there are

Table 1 The Role of Social Media in Museums

References	Research objective	Methodology	Role of social media
(López et al, 2010)	To explore the extent to which Web 2.0 tools are being used by museums on their websites	Analysis of 240 museum websites belonging to four categories (arts, natural sciences, social sciences, and specialized)	The availability of Web 2.0 tools in museum websites is still very rare. Anglo-Saxon museums have a more extended usage of social media tools, than French, Italian and Spanish museums.
(Mencarelli and Pulh, 2012)	To identify the new roles devoted to museum visitors and to discuss their impacts on museum missions	Careful examination of sites and social media features offered by museums	Social media offer three new roles to museum visitors: • Communication manager • Online curator • Artist
(Proctor, 2010)	To delineate the new role of curators in the age of social media	Conceptual paper	Democratize control of and access to culture
(Russo, 2011)	To understand how the implementation of strategic social media programs can drive online cultural exchange and create new connections with diverse communities	Critical assessments of two examples from the cultural sector: • Global event • Online networking in design	• New forms of innovation (crowdsourcing) • Emergence of design communities • Creative connections
(Russo et al, 2008)	To discuss the potential of social media for retaining and extending museum authority	Conceptual paper	Create or improve popular knowledge sharing networks Provide audiences with a voice, allowing them to participate in cultural debate

three important flows of customer communication and conceptualize the 3-M framework to assess each of these flows of communication:

1. the firm-to-customer communication is named the Megaphone,
2. the customer-to-firm communication is represented by the Magnet and
3. the customer-to-customer interaction is labelled the Monitor.

The 3-M framework was then applied to analyse Starbuck's communication paths.

If we apply the 3-M framework to museums, the Megaphone corresponds to Proctor (2010)'s description of the new role of curators in the age of social media: Curators or museum professionals using social media to communicate with their publics. For instance, the Metropolitan Museum of Art's Web site has an attraction called "Connections," where behind-the-scene staff members talk about their favorite works in the collection. Curators, but also directors of exhibitions share their personal point of views with video and audio testimonies. On the website, it is explained that "their voices range from the authoritative to the highly subjective, and touch upon any number of themes and concepts."[1]

Museums also can use social media like "a Magnet to draw inbound dialog" (Gallaugher and Ransbotham, 2010, p. 200). The participation of online visitors can be used for diverse strategies such as exhibition curation, collections enhancement, community of interest and museum learning (Russo et al, 2008). For instance, the Smithsonian museum extensively relies on crowdsourcing and user-generated content to classify its observations, to identify works of art, and to create online databases. "Philatelic experts around the world can research – and sometimes pinpoint inaccuracies in – the museum's collection." (Olson, 2011).

Nonetheless, Table 1 also indicates that very few empirical studies have examined the effective participation of visitors in museum strategies. A better balance between curators' and visitors' voice is desirable and social media can encourage it, but more research is needed to validate if social media actually contribute to visitors' participation. As a point of fact, López et al (2010) found that the Magnet usage of social media was still rare on French, Italian and Spanish museum websites. These museums tend to have a limited usage of blogs and forums especially, because they consider these sources of knowledge as unauthoritative. Consequently, more research is needed to assess participation profiles of museum visitors with social media.

5 Outlook on Future Research

The survey methodology will be designed to conduct this research. Through online questionnaires with museum visitors, we will try to iden-

---

[1] http://www.metmuseum.org/connections/about-connections

tify different profiles of visitors' participation with social media. Another objective will be to test the Expectation-Confirmation Theory (Bhattacherjee, 2001; Oliver, 1977) in order to determine if visitors' expectations regarding online participation with social media are met when communicating with museums. Our findings can be interesting to researchers who work on social media by providing new insights from the cultural and non-profit sector. This research will also be of interest to museum professionals who have recently discovered the potential of social media but keep using these tools as a Megaphone and ignore the Magnet perspective (i.e. visitors' voice).

References

Bernoff J, Li C (2008) Harnessing the power of the oh-so-social web. MIT Sloan Management Review 49(3):36–42

Bhattacherjee A (2001) Understanding information systems continuance: An expectation-confirmation model. MIS Quarterly 25(3):351–370, DOI 10.2307/3250921

Bloch MJ (2004) The nonprofit status of the museum. ICOM News 57(2):4–5

Burton C, Scott C (2003) Museums: Challenges for the 21st century. International Journal of Arts Management 5(2):56–68

Cameron F (2005) Contentiousness and shifting knowledge paradigms: The roles of history and science museums in contemporary societies. Museum Management and Curatorship 20(3):213–233, DOI 10.1080/09647770500502003

Carr D (2001) A museum is an open work. International Journal of Heritage Studies 7(2):173–183, DOI 10.1080/13527250117281

Dümcke C, Gnedovsky M (2013) The social and economic value of cultural heritage: literature review. EENC Paper

Elliott N, Sverdlov G (2012) Global social media adoption in 2011 - a social computing report. Tech. rep., Forrester

Foster MK, Francescucci A, West BC (2010) Why users participate in online social networks. International Journal of E-business Management 4(1):3–19

France Diplomatie (2006) La france en bref: Culture et loisirs

Gallaugher J, Ransbotham S (2010) Social media and customer dialog management at starbucks. MIS Quarterly Executive 9(4):197–212

Gob A, Drouguet N (2003) La muséologie: Histoire, développements, enjeux actuels. Armand Colin, Paris

Groupe EAC (2011) 150 musées et lieux culturels français face aux innovations technologiques, Paris

Hicks M (2005) 'A whole new world': The young person's experience of visiting Sydney Technological Museum. Museum and Society 3(2):66–80

Hooper-Greenhill E (2000) Changing values in the art museum: Rethinking communication and learning. International Journal of Heritage Studies 6(1):9–31, DOI 10.1080/135272500363715

ICOM   (2002)   ICOM   Statutes.   URL   http://icom.museum/statutes.html#2,

Kaplan AM, Haenlein M (2010) Users of the world, unite! The challenges and opportunities of social media. Business Horizons 53(1):59–68

Lochon PY (2012) Musées mondiaux et réseaux sociaux / TOP 50 / Février 2012. Club Innovation et Culture France, Paris

López X, Margapoti I, Maragliano R, Bove G (2010) The presence of web 2.0 tools on museum websites: A comparative study between England, France, Spain, Italy, and the USA. Museum Management and Curatorship 25(2):235–249

Mencarelli R, Pulh M (2012) Web 2.0 et musées: Les nouveaux visages du visiteur. Décisions marketing 65:77–82

Oliver RL (1977) Effect of expectation and disconfirmation on postexposure product evaluations - an alternative interpretation. Journal of Applied Psychology 62(4):480–486

Olson E (2011) Smithsonian uses social media to expand its mission. New York Times, 2011-16-03

Porter M (2006) Strategy for Museums. Harvard Business School, Boston

Proctor N (2010) Digital: Museum as platform, curator as champion, in the age of social media. Curator: The Museum Journal 53(1):35–43

Rieu AM (1988) Les Visiteurs et leurs musées: Le cas des musées de Mulhouse. Documentation française, Paris

Ross M (2004) Interpreting the new museology. Museum and Society 2(2):84–103

Russo A (2011) Transformations in cultural communication: Social media, cultural exchange, and creative connections. Curator: The Museum Journal 54(3):327–346

Russo A, Watkins J, Kelly L, Chan S (2008) Participatory communication with social media. Curator: The Museum Journal 51(1):21–31

Searle A (1984) Museums and the Public Interest. American Association of Museums, Washington, D.C.

Šola T, Museoliitto S (1997) Essays on Museums and Their Theory: Towards the Cybernetic Museum. Museological publications, Finnish Museums Association, Helsinki

Uriely N (2005) The tourist experience: Conceptual developments. Annals of Tourism Research 32(1):199–216, DOI 10.1016/j.annals.2004.07.008

Zorloni A (2012) Designing a strategic framework to assess museum activities. International Journal of Arts Management 14(2):31–72

What's New With You? On the Moderating Effect of Product Novelty on eWOM Effectiveness

Daria Plotkina and Andreas Munzel

Abstract With the growing importance of the Internet and its increasing impact on everyday behaviour and consumption practices, online recommendations by other consumers are of great importance. As a major source of web-accessible information, prior research provides support for the role online reviews play in consumers' decision-making processes. Our research investigates the thus far, understudied effect of novelty on the effectiveness of e-recommendations via online reviews. We conduct a multi-categorical study integrating the moderating effect of product novelty on the recommendation receiver's purchase intention after exposure to a positive or negative online review. We find that new products are indeed less appealing and more impacted by online reviews, but only for products that are purchased frequently enough to distinguish between new and old ones. On the other hand, products that are less familiar to the customer are all the same new to him whether they were launched on the market recently or a long time ago. Our study contributes to the growing field of online word-of-mouth behaviour research by investigating the role of novelty in several product categories.

Daria Plotkina
EM Strasbourg Business School, HuManiS, University of Strasbourg, 61 Avenue de la Forêt Noire, 67085 Strasbourg Cedex, France
✉ daria.plotkina@em-strasbourg.eu

Andreas Munzel
EM Strasbourg Business School, HuManiS, University of Strasbourg, 61 Avenue de la Forêt Noire, 67085 Strasbourg Cedex, France
✉ andreas.munzel@em-strasbourg.eu

CUSTOMER & SERVICE SYSTEMS
KIT SCIENTIFIC PUBLISHING
Vol. 1, No. 1, S. 103–114, 2014

DOI 10.5445/KSP/1000038784/12
ISSN 2198-8005
(cc) BY-SA

1 Purpose and Background of the Research

1.1 Impact of electronic word-of-mouth on purchase decision

The Internet opens new opportunities for consumers to conduct pre-purchase information searches (Brown et al, 2007) and they become increasingly dependent on it to find the information they need (Bagozzi and Dholakia, 2002; Brown et al, 2007). Consumers often ask the advice of people around them, i.e. friends, opinion leaders, expert consumers or even individuals combining these characteristics (Bertrandias and Vernette, 2012). Despite the still powerful role of personal communication in shaping consumers' opinion and decision, the rapid development of the Internet in recent years has encouraged peer consumer online interaction or electronic word-of-mouth (eWOM) (Cheung et al, 2008). Additionally, under certain circumstances (online business, geographical distance, rare expertise, and budget limitation) e-marketing is the only feasible option, both for companies and consumers. As consumers increasingly exchange and rely on opinions and experiences regarding products and services shared via eWOM (Bagozzi and Dholakia, 2002), eWOM becomes an important communication tool for marketers.

Empirical research shows the impact of eWOM on sales (Zhu and Zhang, 2010), purchasing intentions (Park et al, 2007), and product choice (Senecal and Nantel, 2004). There is no doubt left that eWOM heavily impacts consumers' purchasing behaviour and attitudes toward brands, products, services, and companies. However, there are many factors that influence this impact. These factors have been researched from different points of view: based on the nature of eWOM (Chiou and Cheng, 2003), based on the platform where it is published (Brown et al, 2007), quantity and quality of reviews, reviewed product (movies: Chakravarty et al (2010); hotels: Kim et al (2011)), and characteristics of the reviewer (e.g. gender: Kim et al, 2011).

Our literature review shows that the majority of empirical studies in the field of eWOM effectiveness concentrate only on one type of product and/or service neglecting the role of the product and/or service category by including this aspect. However, a few studies in traditional word-of-mouth (WOM) communication that integrated several product categories were able to show differences in WOM effectiveness (East et al, 2008). We, therefore, included several product categories to examine its importance in the online environment.

Furthermore, we identified a gap in the literature concerning the impact of the novelty of the product on eWOM effectiveness.

1.2 Importance of product novelty in eWOM effectiveness

We believe that with the growing importance of innovation and the difficulty for an innovation to succeed on the market, the possible dependence of the reaction to eWOM on the novelty of the reviewed service and/or product is of paramount interest. Unceasingly there are new launched products and services on the market. Innovation is crucial for business survival, as improving and developing service operations is expected to lead to growth and differentiation of service quality, reduced costs and greater responsiveness (Simchi-Levi, 2010).

According to a theoretical and empirical review by Herbig and Day (1992) the customers' awareness and the implication in the innovation increase the acceptance of the product, however, few approaches emphasize the importance of information diffusion and right communication with the consumers. As a result many companies do not adopt their practices and bear losses when launching a new offer.

Originally though, early investigations in the field of WOM behaviour highlighted the importance of interpersonal influence and customer-to-customer interactions in the diffusion and, therefore, success of innovations in the market (e.g. Arndt, 1967). In this early stream of literature dedicated to interpersonal communication and consumers' recommendation behaviour, WOM is perceived as a measure to diffuse innovations and, therefore, crucial for its success (Arndt, 1967). However, whereas prior studies researched a wide range of eWOM attributes, the relevance of product novelty has so far been neglected. In this study we only analyze the novelty effect for the same product, however, we are ambitious to continue to further investigate the question by bringing radical innovations into the picture.

As a consequence, the goal of the paper is to learn about the effect of product novelty on the impact of eWOM on the receiver's purchase decision. We investigate three main relations: (1) overall product novelty influence on the eWOM impact on purchase decision; (2) interaction of novelty, eWOM valence, and the impact on purchase decision; and (3) interaction of novelty and product category in eWOM impact on the decision to buy.

2 Hypotheses

Attitude-formation theories, such as the Elaboration-Likelihood Model (ELM) (Cacioppo and Petty, 1986) and the Heuristic-Systematic Processing Model (HSM) (Chaiken, 1980), suggest that consumer experience or knowledge is a key variable in the formation of attitude. Lack of product-specific knowledge and insufficient information are perceived as risk. Researchers agree that overall the greater the perceived risk is, the less likely the product will be purchased (Ross, 1975). Based on the very definition, novelty captures a very important notion of risk related to the product. Consistent with existing conceptual and empirical studies in eWOM impact on the intention to buy and the above-mentioned theory on the perceived risk and purchase decision, we expect the influence of online reviews to be greater on "new" products than on "old" products <Hypothesis 1>.

Furthermore, existing research shows convincing evidence that negative online reviews have a wider impact than the positive ones (Fiske, 1992; Chiou and Cheng, 2003). We expect this relation to be enhanced by the novelty factor in a way that it will intensify the relative impact of negative eWOM over positive eWOM for the new offers <Hypothesis 2>.

Numerous empirical studies have proved differences in the eWOM effect on products of different categories (Verhagen et al, 2010; Park et al, 2007). In accordance with these studies we expect a significant difference among the reviews impact on the three products <Hypothesis 3>.

3 Method

3.1 Experimental design and procedure

We conduct a 2 (product novelty: new vs. old) x 3 (type of product: restaurant, mobile package, car repairs) x 2 (eWOM valence: positive vs. negative) experiment using a between-subject factorial design. This matrix is divided into several smaller studies for every product: first investigating the novelty effect and then adding other variables to check for correlations and compound effects.

Online reviews were used to manipulate the valence of the reviews. These re-views posted by other consumers were preceded by a brief product description and short promotional offer manipulating product novelty and the type of the product. The 3 types of the products were chosen to be different based on several classifications (see Table 1). The product type impacts the type of information that is requested and its effectiveness (Verhagen et al, 2010). We concentrated on services, as they are more likely to be checked upon with eWOM information, being of a more intangible and heterogeneous nature (Huang et al, 2007). Based on previous research (e.g. Cheung et al, 2008; East et al, 2008) and the characteristics of the product (frequently purchased and viewed/ reviewed, accessible for everyone, bearing moderate consequences etc.) the main product is a restaurant. Whereas the respective product or service is already existent in the market for several years, the offering is completely new to the market in opposite novelty manipulation. Consistent with prior research, we explore the eWOM impact by taking into account the importance of the valence of the online review (Fiske, 1992; Chiou and Cheng, 2003): Positive eWOM (PWOM) and negative eWOM (NWOM) were used for satisfactory and unsatisfactory experiences by the eWOM senders respectively.

As being potential influencing factors, first, we controlled for the respondent's experiences with this form of eWOM and his general tendency to buy new products before other consumers by including Internet experience and familiarity as well as the individual innovativeness (Midgley and Dowling, 1978) in the first part of the questionnaire. In a second step, the respondent is exposed to an offer and is asked to evaluate the offer attractiveness to control for unintended effects in our study. After presenting a negative or a positive online review in the next step, we checked for the success of our manipulations and measured the dependent variable, purchase intention. A control group was not exposed to the online reviews and was asked to evaluate their purchase intention based on the described product offer. Finally, we checked for ecological validity and collected socio-demographical parameters of the respondents.

3.2 Measures

The measures have been taken primarily from existing research and respondents answered on 7-point Likert scales from 1 "totally disagree" to 7 "totally agree". Measures for the consumer's innovativeness were compiled from scales suggested by Roehrich (1995) and Le Louarn (1997). Three statements to evaluate the attractiveness of the offer were adapted from the scale for the attitude towards the product used by Lepkowska-White et al (2003). Items to measure the respondent's purchase intention were adapted from Chandran and Morwitz (2005) as well as Dodds et al (1991). Three items from Bradley and Sparks (2009) were used to check the realism of the scenario and the respondent's ability to put himself into the described situation. To check whether the manipulations on eWOM valence and the product category relative to the SEC framework worked out as intended, we included two single items asking for the respondent's perception of the positivity of the review and his appraisal whether the product quality can be evaluated easily or not.

3.3 Sampling

Participants were recruited evenly from social networks, by email and with the help of amazon mechanical turk. The questionnaires were anonymous and automatically randomized. Lately, amazon turk was confirmed to provide valid and reliable results (Rand, 2012): apparently, the online engine enables cross-cultural studies even better than other ways of respondents recruitment. We therefore assume that the sample is valid and sufficiently big (1564 respondents after all checks and clearings) to yield solid results.

4 Results

We have validated our Hypothesis 1 for the main product: new restaurants were viewed less appealing and were more impacted by eWOM. We have partially validated our Hypothesis 2 stating that negative reviews have a significantly greater impact on the purchase intention than the positive ones, but this influence does not depend on the product novelty. Validation of Hypothesis 3 brought us some very interesting insight into the correlation of product type and product novelty. All the three products showed a significantly different impact in the light of the eWOM displayed to the respondents (p-value>0,01). As the restaurant was the only product the evaluation of which depended on the novelty and taking in count the characteristics of the studied product we could conclude that products that are not frequently purchased by the consumers are not familiar and thus are new as a whole class of products to the consumer, with no regard for the exact launch of the product on the market. Also we could state the importance of a multi-categorical study to yield general result or, on the other hand, a need to conduct a narrowly specialized study for one (type of) product for more precise conclusions.

We have validated our Hypothesis 1 reversely and only for the main product: new restaurants were viewed less appealing and were significantly ($p <, 001$) less impacted by positive eWOM (see Figure 1). We have partially validated our Hypothesis 2 stating that negative reviews have a significantly greater impact on the purchase intention than the positive ones (see Figure 2), but this influence does not depend on the product novelty. As expected in Hypothesis 3, the findings show that eWOM effectiveness differs respective to product categories: we observe significant differences of the effect of eWOM on purchase intention across the three product types in our study ($F = 2, 13; p <, 1$). As the restaurant was the only product the evaluation of which depended on the novelty and taking in count the characteristics of the studied product we could conclude that products that are not frequently purchased by the consumers are not familiar and thus are new as a whole class of products to the consumer, with no regard for the exact launch of the product on the market. Also we could state the importance of a multi-categorical study to yield general result or, on the other hand, a need to conduct a narrowly specialized study for one (type of) product for more precise conclusions.

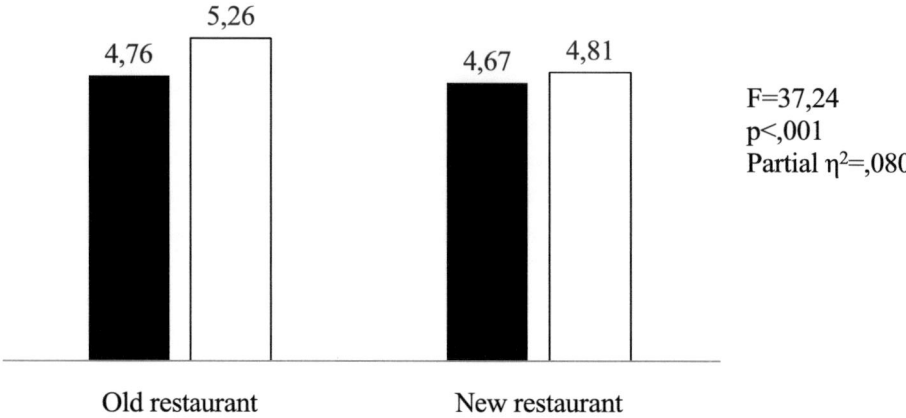

Fig. 1 Impact of positive online reviews on purchase intention of restaurant: Novelty factor (H1)

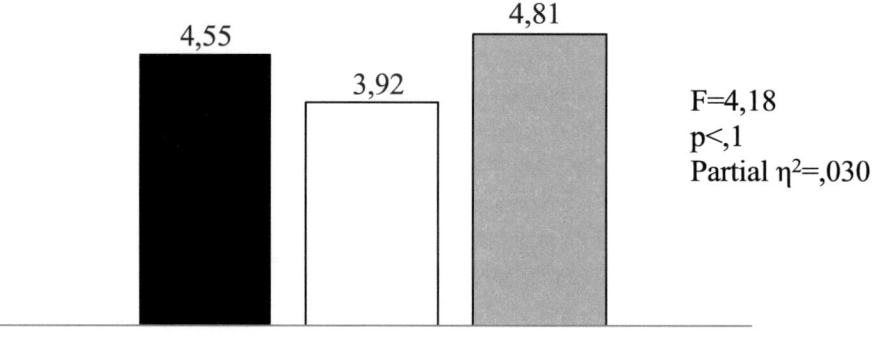

Fig. 2 Impact of online reviews on the purchase intention: Aggregated means (H2)

5 Discussions and Implications

Our research investigates the important question of the novelty effect on eWOM impact on the purchase decision. In a way we come back to the initial purpose of WOM in the diffusion of new products and fill in the existing research gap with regard to novelty. It is important to see if with the immense volume of online information, its speed and accessibility, the novelty of a product has a stand-alone impact on the eWOM effectiveness, interacts with other product-specific factors or does not play any significant role in influencing the online reviews impact on the purchase decision.

Launching new products and managing them is indisputably important in the modern world: We propose that knowing eWOM dependence on the novelty of the goods might be considered as a contribution to improve managerial practices. Beyond any doubt eWOM influences purchase decisions. With the increased importance of purchases and a more significant impact of eWOM for new products on the market, companies should pay attention to online consumer reviews in order to support the launched products. Managers should encourage consumers to write online reviews to attract further customers throughout all the life cycle of the product. Additionally, even more effort should be made to deal with negative reviews; keeping in mind that negative eWOM has a deeper impact on purchase decision. The novelty factor plays an additional moderating role on the importance of eWOM for products that are frequently purchased.

Undeniably, the study has very distinct limitations: the number of products, the number of reviews, the abridged language of reviews, and the approach to the product novelty. We believe that this topic could be interesting to the re-searchers and managers by integrating new angles such as radical innovations and reviews by experts and innovators with a too specific vocabulary for the regular consumer to understand.

Table 1 The List of Used Products and their Characteristics

Char./Product	Mobile package	Restaurant	Car repairs
Type (SEC)	search	experience	credence
Hedonic/ utilitarian	utilitarian	hedonic	utilitarian
Frequency of purchase	once in a while	often	exceptional purchase
Long-lasting consequences	possibly	no	yes
Related costs	average	moderate	substantial
Perceived responsibility	average	low	high
Acquaintance	moderate	high	low
Novelty definition	classic / new	well known / just opened	factory-based garage / newly opened garage
Comments	one company in order to reduce risk and uncertainty of a new provider: provider is known and info on the package is stated and clear		

References

Arndt J (1967) Role of product-related conversations in the diffusion of a new product. Journal of Marketing Research 4(3):291–295

Bagozzi R, Dholakia U (2002) Intentional social action in virtual communities. Journal of Interactive Marketing 16(2):2–21

Bertrandias L, Vernette É (2012) What is interpersonal communication worth? Interpersonal calibration of knowledge and selection of recommendation sources. Recherche et Applications en Marketing 27(1):33–56

Bradley GL, Sparks BA (2009) Dealing with service failures: The use of explanations. Journal of Travel & Tourism Marketing 26(2):129–143

Brown J, Broderick AJ, Lee N (2007) Word of mouth communication within online communities: Conceptualizing the online social network. Journal of Interactive Marketing 21(3):2–20

Cacioppo JT, Petty RE (1986) Psychology: Systems, processes, and applications, social processes in M.G.H. Guildford, New York

Chaiken S (1980) Heuristic versus systematic information processing and the use of source versus message cues in persuasion. Journal of Personality and Social Psychology 39(5):752–766

Chakravarty A, Liu Y, Mazumdar T (2010) The differential effects of online word-of-mouth and critics' reviews on pre-release movie evaluation. Journal of Interactive Marketing 24(3):185–197

Chandran S, Morwitz VG (2005) Effects of participative pricing on consumers' cognitions and actions: A goal theoretic perspective. Journal of Consumer Research 32(2):249–259

Cheung CM, Lee MK, Rabjohn N (2008) The impact of electronic word-of-mouth: The adoption of online opinions in online customer communities. Internet Research 18(3):229–247

Chiou JS, Cheng C (2003) Should a company have message boards on its web sites? Journal of Interactive Marketing 17(3):50–61

Dodds WB, Monroe KB, Grewal D (1991) Effects of price, brand, and store information on buyers' product evaluations. Journal of Marketing Research 28(3):307–319

East R, Hammond K, Lomax W (2008) Measuring the impact of positive and negative word of mouth on brand purchase probability. International Journal of Research in Marketing 25(3):215–224

Fiske ST (1992) Thinking is for doing: Portraits of social cognition from daguerreotype to laserphoto. Journal of Personality and Social Psychology 63(6):877–889

Herbig PA, Day RL (1992) Customer acceptance: the key to successful introductions of innovations. Marketing Intelligence & Planning 10(1):4–15

Huang LS, Chou YJ, Lan IT (2007) Effects of perceived risk, message types, and reading motives on the acceptance and transmission of electronic word-of-mouth communication. Contemporary Management Research 3(4):299–312

Kim EEK, Mattila AS, Baloglu S (2011) Effects of gender and expertise on consumers' motivation to read online hotel reviews. Cornell Hospitality Quarterly 52(4):399–406

Le Louarn P (1997) La tendance á innover des consommateurs: Analyse conceptuelle et proposition d'une èchelle de mesure. Recherche et Applications en Marketing 12(1):3–19

Lepkowska-White E, Brashear TG, Weinberger MG (2003) A test ad appeal effectiveness in poland and the united states: The interplay of appeal, product, and culture. Journal of Advertising 32(3):57–67

Midgley DF, Dowling GR (1978) Innovativeness: The concept and its measurement. Journal of Consumer Research 4(4):229–242

Park DH, Lee J, Han I (2007) The effect of on-line consumer reviews on consumer purchasing intention: The moderating role of involvement. International Journal of Electronic Commerce 11(4):125–148

Rand DG (2012) The promise of mechanical turk: How online labor markets can help theorists run behavioral experiments. Journal of Theoretical Biology 299:172–179

Roehrich G (1995) Innovativités hédoniste et sociale: Proposition d'une échelle de mesure. Recherche et Applications en Marketing 9(2):19–42

Ross I (1975) Perceived risk and consumer behavior: A critical review. Advances in Consumer Research Volume 2:1–20

Senecal S, Nantel J (2004) The influence of online product recommendations on consumers' online choices. Journal of Retailing 80(2):159–169

Simchi-Levi D (2010) Operations Rules: Delivering Customer Value Through Flexible Operations. Mit, Cambridge, MA

Verhagen T, Boter J, Adelaar T (2010) The effect of product type on consumer preferences for website content elements: An empirical study. Journal of Computer-Mediated Communication 16(1):139–170

Zhu F, Zhang XM (2010) Impact of online consumer reviews on sales: The moderating role of product and consumer characteristics. Journal of Marketing 74(2):133–148

e-Voicing an Opinion on a Brand – A Research Agenda

Claire Roederer and Marc Filser

1 Online practices of consumers and cyber-experiences

"Markets are conversations". With this first suggestion and the 94 others that followed, the authors of the Cluetrain manifesto (Levine et al, 2000) highlighted in 1999, the fundamental changes that the advent of the Internet would generate in the manner of considering the relationship to markets and more generally speaking commercial exchanges. They emphasize in particular, the progressive replacement of traditional mass-marketing tools by the generalisation of a new means of communication characterised by novel forms of conversation between consumers on the one side and companies and their brands on the other.

Consumers expect greater transparency, authenticity, reactiveness, options and support by the company with regard to its responsibilities in relation to them and to society in general (Myron, 2010). Consumers strong reactions to Sony *"AllIwantforXmasispsp"* campaign in 2006 show how consumers can fiercely reject a brand that created a fake consumer blog to promote itself. Thanks to the Internet, consumers have the means to

Claire Roederer
Associate Professor of Marketing, EM Strasbourg (laboratoire HuManiS), Université de Strasbourg
✉ claire.roederer@em-strasbourg.eu

Marc Filser
Full Professor of Marketing, IAE de Dijon (laboratoire LEG-Cermab, UMR 5118), Université de Bourgogne
✉ marc.filser@u-bourgogne.fr

CUSTOMER & SERVICE SYSTEMS
KIT SCIENTIFIC PUBLISHING
Vol. 1, No. 1, S. 115–125, 2014

DOI 10.5445/KSP/1000038784/13
ISSN 2198-8005

be treated not as mere numbers, but as individuals to be heard. In other words, thanks to information technologies, they can enjoy new forms of power/control. The Internet is, in fact, considered as an empowerment tool both in the field of consumer behaviour and in information systems, to the extent that it allows consumers to interact with the rest of the world at different levels (personal, dyad, group, community) (Amichai-Hamburger, 2008). Yet, consumers are not all equal in relation to these new uses and to the potential power they wield (Kozinets, 2008).

However, the different ways in which this power available to the consumer can be expressed is to be found in new practices in the form of cyber experiences.

Cyber experiences or on-line experiences are defined as all the consumer experiences, i.e. interactions of person × object × situation (Punj and Stewart, 1983) which generate significance for the persons experiencing them (Filser, 2002, 2008), whether such interactions are market or non-market related. Cyber experiences presuppose an human-computer interaction, and can take place in any real physical or virtual place and concern any product or service category (Kozinets, 2002).

1.1 Categories of cyber experiences

1.1.1 Market cyber experiences (in a narrow sense)

This type of interaction covers online shopping experiences (Soopramanien, 2011), and corresponds to shopping experiences (Tauber, 1972) in conventional shops / stores selling goods and services. By cutting the storage and distribution costs, the Internet allows several companies to market products that would not be economically viable in conventional stores, thus resulting in an almost unlimited increase in offers (Anderson, 2006).

1.1.2 Market and non-market cyber experiences

In addition to the market cyber experiences described above, these include:

The search for information experience. The search experience comes prior to the buying and consumption experience (Arnould et al, 2002). The search for information, which has become extremely intuitive through the use of engines such as Google (Battelle, 2005), is one of the activities most shared by web users. We could even maintain that the search for information is the starting point of any cyber-experience. Clemons (2008) believes that the information the web user is likely to obtain with just a few clicks, affects his behaviour and consequently, all the variables in a classic marketing mix. The search for information varies according to product category (e.g. search vs. experience products) (Nelson, 1970) and focuses on price and product information from various sources (websites advertising, business and retailer websites, as well as consumer generated product reviews available through online newsgroups, communities or chatrooms).

Entertainment experiences. The Internet could be considered as a source of entertainment, with unspecified borders, in which the web user can enjoy an infinite number of recreational and/or instructive experiences (Addis, 2005).

Content creation experiences. These involve the production/circulation of content in chat rooms, forums, blogs, or on a wider scale, the experience of the presence more or less active on social networks like Facebook. The experience of "voicing an opinion" and the resulting discourse could relate to any consumer/brand interaction (having taken place on the Internet or in real life), whether real or fictional. These comprise experiences resulting in the production of a consumer generated content (Fournier and Brunel, 2008). It should be noted that consumers not only generate comments but also products and services. Threadless company is a good example of consumers efforts to create designs for Tshirts sold online (Howe, 2008). Whereas Zagat guides, a world's leading provider of consumer survey-based information for restaurants and other leisure activities, offer an illustration of the power of consumer generated reviews in more than 100 countries worldwide.

1.2 Cyber-experiences involving brands

If we focus on cyber-experiences involving brands, two major categories
of practices can be distinguished:

1. Practices implying consumer generated content as regards the brand;
2. Practices directly linked to a phase of the decision making process
   involved in buying the brand.

1.2.1 Content generation for a brand

Consumer generated content for a brand can take different forms. The
content could be a commentary, a recommendation, a rate, tag, comment,
blog, tweet, friend (Hardey, 2011) with the purpose of providing information to others which then becomes eWOM. But the content generated for
the brand could go as far as the creation of an advertisement referred
to as consumer generated advertising (Campbell et al, 2011), the brand
parody (Fournier and Avery, 2011) or the generation of ideas for brands
(crowdsourcing) (Howe, 2008).

1.2.2 Practices directly linked to the buying process

These cyber experiences impact one or several of the phases of the
decision-making process when buying. It can be considered that the tools
proposed in the Internet are used by consumers for strategic purposes to
optimize information on the product or even to increase their power of
negotiation in relation to the company and consequently to gain control
or counter balance control attributed to the company (Fig. 2).

2 Research orientation

2.1 Grid of reasons and forms of voicing an opinion online

Fournier and Avery (2011) speak of *Open Source Branding* in relation to
the observable mechanisms/practices on the Internet which involve the

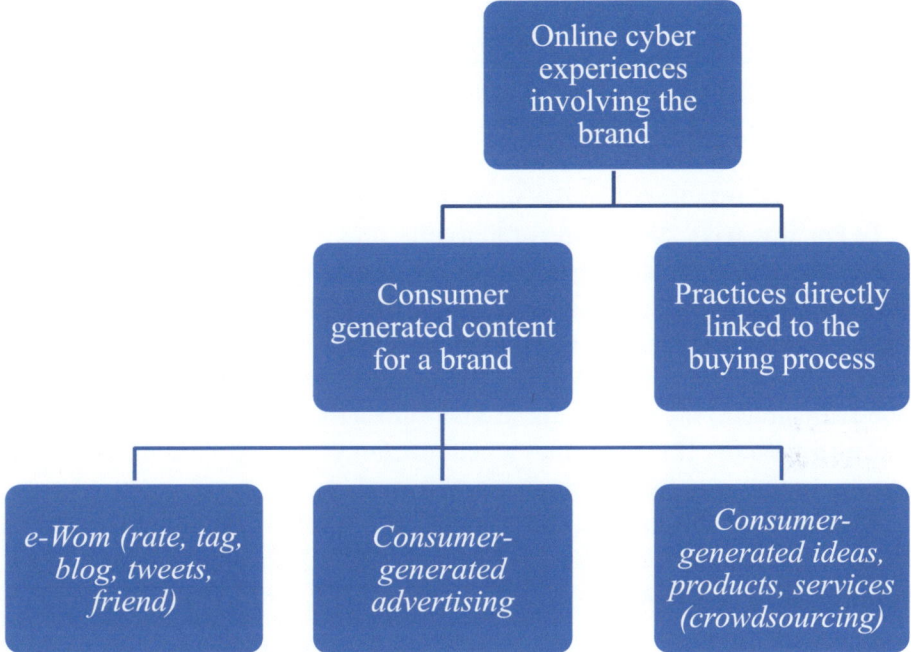

Fig. 1 Content generation for a brand

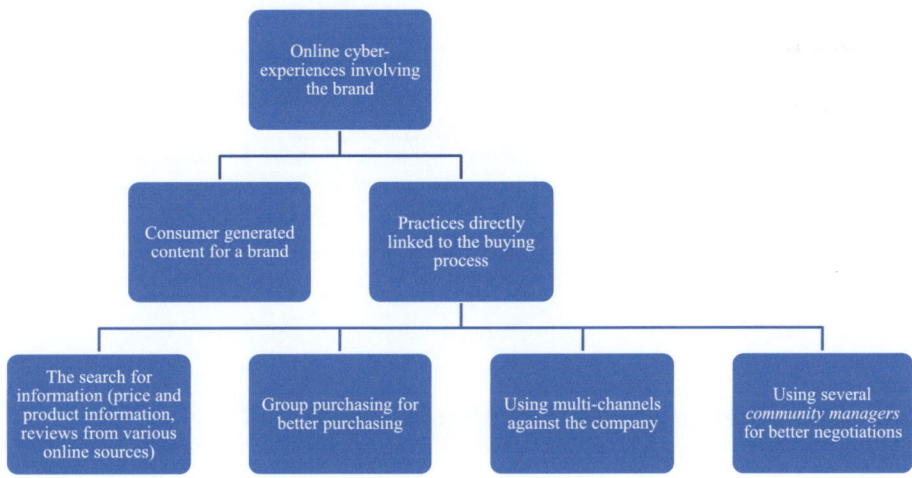

Fig. 2 Cyber-experiences affecting the buying process

web user and the brand. After having identified four themes underlying these practices (*the age of social collective, the age of transparency, the age of criticism, the age of parody*) and three lines of corporate behavior in response (*the path of least resistance, playing their game, leveraging Web 2.0 interconnectedness*), Fournier and Avery contend that the observed practices call into question the paradigm of brand management.

In keeping with the finding of Fournier and Avery (2011), the grid (Table 1) explores the elements potentially underlying the online opinion statements of consumers regarding a brand/company. This grid is structured around the context of voicing an opinion by characterizing it in relation to an element triggering the opinion statement (transaction vs. non transaction) on the one hand and characterizing the context by taking into account the consumer's orientation (cooperative/conflictual). It results in four quadrants which we will analyze.

Among the different research themes of interest to us, we will focus on those suggested by Fournier and Brunel (2008), corresponding to quadrants 1 and 2 of Table 1.

Table 1 Grid for structuring forms of online opinion statements

		Consumer orientation in relation to the brand	
		Cooperative	Conflictual
Context of consumer voicing an opinion	Linked to a transaction	1. Communication of information Recommendation Product review	3.Claim using competition/opportunism
	Independent of a transaction	2. Tribal belonging / fan club Recommendation On-line communities, fan pages, CGA	4. Protestation Boycott / disparagement Voice/exit

2.2 Consumer-generated content for a brand

Consumers as 'translators' and 'co-creators' of meaning: Is this new role a source of value? Market surveys show the high level of acceptance by consumers of information provided in the Internet by other customers, and research has highlighted the role actually played by this kind of information in the consumer decision process. If the benefits of consumer-generated information to other consumers are well documented, less attention has been devoted to the benefits that a consumer can find in this process of information generation. A reference to the opinion leadership literature is a first track of investigation, even though the e-opinion leader may capture significantly different forms of recognition in the Internet, when compared with the "classical" forms of opinion leadership in a "real world" social circle.

Are consumers who generate content for a brand more likely to adopt one of the identified practices directly linked to the buying process?

What variables can best explain the adoption of practices such as content generation, or practices directly linked to the buying process?

Can the proposed categorization serve as a sound basis to develop consumer typologies?

Does consumer generated advertising (CGA) present a fundamentally different advertising paradigm or does it operate to persuade in the same way as company-sponsored advertising? The same market surveys signal a potential gap between the credibility of company sponsored information, and consumer generated information in the Internet. Whereas banners, pop ups and other familiar communication supports are perceived as intrusive and generate negative comments, consumer generated information systematically receives a more positive assessment. How will these contrasted effects impact the role of different sources in the consumer decision process? Will consumer generated content become a new source of consumer empowerment and lead to a significant shift in the balance of power in the marketplace? Or will the brands be able to keep control over those new means of expression? These questions are decisive in order to better understand the future shape of relations in the marketplace.

2.3 Active Internet user behavior pattern overtime

There is a strong need to investigate the link between consumer expression on the web and consumer behavior. For example, are very "loud" consumers more loyal to the brand over time than less active customers? The extreme case of the brand tribe has been analyzed by European and north American field works, and exemplifies a very intense link between voice and action. But it is dubious to consider that every consumer posting information on the web is a passionate member of the brand community (Füller et al, 2008).

A parallel may be drawn with the results of research exploring the link between satisfaction / dissatisfaction and brand loyalty. Some dissatisfied consumers may become very loyal buyers of the brand if the motives of their dissatisfaction have been solved by the brand. Do such traits operate on the web? Maybe a dissatisfied consumer will post information on a forum, get involved in an intense exchange of information with other customers, and revise his former negative attitude toward the brand, leading perhaps to the diffusion of more positive information later.

Using longitudinal data on e-voicing, and linking this data with actual buying behavior, could provide useful cues to better assess links between speech and action.

2.4 Firms' stances in reaction to Internet users voices

Finally, this research should address a managerial question: How should a company take into account a typology of Internet users based on "voicing styles"? Should this variable be measured (and how?) and integrated in consumer databases? The recognition of the critical role of consumer involvement in information processing has led brands to radically contrasted persuasive strategies when they address low or high involvement segments. Should voicing styles be taken into account in the same way? And how effective (and efficient) are different answer strategies?

To conclude, we would like to stress the radical change that is occurring in the marketplace due to the development of consumer expression in the Internet. Theoretical analyses of this behavior might be located along a continuum. On the one hand, e-voicing is reflecting a massive rejection of the consumption society, and a sign of some kind of consumer revolution of the "reclaim the streets" style. Such forms of expressions probably exist. But on the other hand, e-voicing may reflect a basic need of the contemporary consumer to get in touch with other people, and to be considered for some kind of expertise he is detaining. And between those extremes, we could imagine a large variety of motives, some basically utilitarian and opportunistic, some more altruistic in essence, reflecting an authentic willingness to share the knowledge and the experience with others.

This research project should rely on a large variety of theoretical frames, from an individualistic psychological frame, to broader schemes derived from the consumer culture theory. And before empirical measures are developed to attempt consumer typologies, a massive qualitative exploratory research should be led to give more substance to the research propositions formulated in this paper.

References

Addis M (2005) New technologies and cultural consumption - edutainment is born! European Journal of Marketing 39(7–8):729–736

Amichai-Hamburger Y (2008) Internet empowerment. Computers in Human Behavior 24(5):1773–1775

Anderson C (2006) The Long Tail: Why the Future of Business is Selling Less of More. Hyperion, New York

Areddy JT (2006) Chinese consumers overwhelm retailers with team tactics. Wall Street Journal Feb, 28

Arnould EJ, Price L, Zinkhan GM (2002) Consumers. McGraw-Hill, New York

Battelle J (2005) The search: How Google and its rivals rewrote the rules of business and transformed our culture. Portfolio, New York

Campbell C, Pitt LF, Parent M, Berthon PR (2011) Understanding consumer conversations around ads in a web 2.0 world. Journal of Advertising 40(1):87–102

Clemons EK (2008) How information changes consumer behavior and how consumer behavior determines corporate strategy. Journal of Management Information Systems 25(2):13–40

Dellarocas C (2003) The digitization of word of mouth: Promise and challenges of online feedback mechanisms. Management Science 49(10):1407–1424

Filser M (2002) Le marketing de la production d'expérience: Statut théorique et implications managériales. Décisions Marketing 28:13–22

Filser M (2008) L'expérience de consommation: concepts, modèles et enjeux managériaux. Recherche et Applications en Marketing 23(3):1–4

Fournier S, Avery J (2011) The uninvited brand. Business Horizons 54(3):193–207

Fournier S, Brunel F (2008) Exploring the evolving terrain of consumer-generated brand content. In: Lee AY, Soman D (eds) Advances in Consumer Research, Association for Consumer Research, vol 35, pp 209–212

Füller J, Matzler K, Hoppe M (2008) Brand community members as a source of innovation. Journal of Product Innovation Management 25(6):608–619

Gupta P, Harris J (2010) How e-wom recommendations influence product consideration and quality of choice: A motivation to process information perspective. Journal of Business Research 63(9–10):1041–1049

Hardey M (2011) To spin straw into gold? New lessons from consumer-generated content. International Journal of Market Research 53(1):13–15

Howe J (2008) Crowdsourcing: Why the Power of the Crowd is Driving the Future of Business. Three Rivers Press, New York

Kozinets RV (2002) The field behind the screen: Using netnography for marketing research in online communities. Journal of Marketing Research 39(1):61–72

Kozinets RV (2008) Technology/ideology: How ideological fields influence consumers' technology narratives. Journal of Consumer Research 34(6):865–881

Kozinets RV, De Valck K, Wojnicki AC, Wilner SJS (2010) Networked narratives: Understanding word-of-mouth marketing in online communities. Journal of Marketing 74(2):71–89

Levine R, Locke C, Searls D, Weinberger D (2000) The Cluetrain Manifesto: The End of Business As Usual. Perseus, Cambridge

Myron D (2010) Customers in the cockpit (editorial). CRM Magazine

Nelson P (1970) Information and consumer behavior. Journal of Political Economy 78(2):311–329

Punj GN, Stewart DW (1983) An interaction framework of consumer decision making. Journal of Consumer Research 10(2):181–196

Rohrbeck R, Steinhoff F, Perder F (2010) Sourcing innovation from your customer: How multinational enterprises use web platforms for virtual customer integration. Technology Analysis & Strategic Management 22(2):117–131

Soopramanien D (2011) Conflicting attitudes and scepticism towards online shopping: The role of experience. International Journal of Consumer Studies 35(3):338–347

Tauber EM (1972) Why do people shop? Journal of Marketing 36(4):46–49

Wang J, Zhao X (2009) Team purchase: Consumer empowerment through collective actions. In: McGill AL, Shavitt S (eds) Advances in Consumer Research, Association for Consumer Research, vol 36, pp 931–932

The Contribution of Gratitude to Satisfaction Models for Complaining Customers

Françoise Simon, Chantal Connan Ghesquiere and Vesselina Tossan

Abstract Consumer research has shown that satisfaction with complaint handling strongly influences word of mouth behaviour, but affects to a lesser extent repurchase intent. To better explain the performance outcomes derived from complaint handling, we propose a conceptual model in which gratitude along with satisfaction are assumed to be critical mediators of the effects of recovery investments on performance outcomes. This model was tested using a quasi-experimental survey drawing on data from multiple industries. Our results show an opposing pattern of results for each mediator. Whereas gratitude strongly influences repurchase intent, but is not related to word of mouth, satisfaction with complaint handling exhibits a high contribution to word of mouth and no significant effect on repurchase intent. Our findings suggest that the mediating role of gratitude and satisfaction rely on different psychological mechanisms. Overall, the research empirically demonstrates that short-term feelings of gratitude generated by a complaint handling act are

Françoise Simon
HuManiS, University of Strasbourg, 61 Avenue de la Forêt Noire, 67085 Strasbourg Cedex, France
✉ francoise.simon@uha.fr

Chantal Connan Ghesquiere
HuManiS (EA 1347), EM Strasbourg Business School – University of Strasbourg
✉ ch.ghesquiere@gmail.com

Vesselina Tossan
HuManis, EM Strasbourg, 61 Avenue de la Forêt Noire, 67085 Strasbourg Cedex, France, Conservatoire National des Arts et Mètiers de Paris.
✉ vesselina.tossan@cnam.fr

CUSTOMER & SERVICE SYSTEMS
KIT SCIENTIFIC PUBLISHING
Vol. 1, No. 1, S. 127–132, 2014

DOI 10.5445/KSP/1000038784/14
ISSN 2198-8005
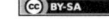

likely to increase purchase intentions. Finally, we draw on the findings of this study to offer implications for service recovery researchers and managers.

1 Introduction and purpose of the research

Reflecting the managerial importance of complaint handling, a large body of research has emphasized the crucial role of transactional satisfaction, which refers to a customer's satisfaction with a complaint handling process. According to this theoretical perspective, transactional satisfaction is assumed to be the main mediator between a company's recovery investments and customers' behaviour. Regarding the consequences of the construct, p revious literature (see for a meta-analysis, Orsingher et al, 2010) has shown that positive word-of-mouth has the highest average correlation among the investigated consequences, confirming the well-known tendency of service customers to share their satisfying or dissatisfying service experience with other people, while the effect on repurchase intent is more tenuous. However, analysis of the underlying mechanisms explaining the weaker influence on repurchase intent is lacking.

Integrating the relationship marketing literature on reciprocity behaviours (e.g. Reynolds and Beatty, 1999; Morales, 2005; Palmatier et al, 2009) with theoretical considerations of transactional satisfaction, the purpose of this research is twofold. First, we propose that the influence of recovery investments on performance outcomes is mediated by both gratitude and satisfaction derived from the complaint-handling process. To our knowledge, the study is the first to address the role of gratitude in the context of complaint handling. While transactional satisfaction reflects the fulfilment of a consumer's expectations in a confirmation/disconfirmation perspective, gratitude is expected to serve as the emotional basis of a complaining consumer's reciprocal behaviours (Palmatier et al, 2009). Second, we rely on a parsimonious model to investigate the contrasting effects of the two mediators. Consistent with Maxham and Netemeyer (2002), we argue that transactional satisfaction prompts customers to tell family and friends about their positive experience primarily due to the salience and recency of the experience, but this is not enough to increase customers' intent to repurchase. Conversely, short-term feelings of gratitude are likely to induce reciprocal behaviours consisting of favours perceived as being particularly valued by companies (e.g. Tsang, 2006), that is, purchase intent. In addition, we postulate that word of mouth intent is an antecedent of repurchase intent, given that individuals tend to behave in accordance with their cognition (e.g. Szymanski and Henard, 2001). Figure 1 shows the hypothesised model for this study.

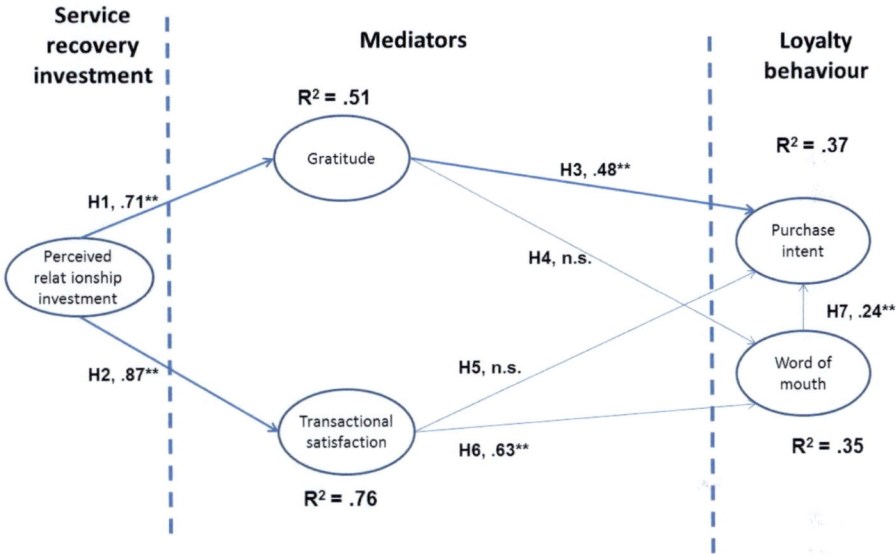

Notes: $^{*}p < .05,$ $^{**}p < .001$, ns not significant, standardised coefficients reported.

Fig. 1 Conceptual model and empirical results

2 Method and results

A survey approach was chosen to examine naturally occurring responses among customers who had recently experienced a service or product failure and a recovery encounter.   Our research design permitted a large variety of sector activities to be represented. Data were collected from a sample of 140 undergraduate business students enrolled in a research methods course. We collected data for our study in two steps. In a first step, students were asked to report any dissatisfaction they experienced

as consumers during one 6-week period. Immediately after performing
their first interaction with the company's customer service, students were
instructed to complete a series of scales designed to assess their perceptions of the complaint handling. Customer service response rates were of
88.6% and 76.1%, respectively, for telephone and online channels. In total, 360 complaints were answered subject to acceptable delay. The scales
used in this research have been elaborated in prior studies that report on
their reliability and validity. We evaluated the psychometric properties
of the constructs by conducting a confirmatory factor analysis (CFA) with
AMOS 19.0. Then, the hypothesised model, as depicted in Figure 1, was
estimated to assess path and explained variance estimates. The model
yielded a good fit while supporting all hypotheses with the exception of
hypotheses H4 and H5, where relationships were found to be not significant. Overall, the model explained 76% of the variance in transactional
satisfaction, 51% in gratitude, 35% in word of mouth and, finally, 37% in
purchase intent. In sum, the hypothesised model was mostly supported
while showing a significant power to explain variance in the final variables. In addition, we investigated the mediating role of both gratitude
and transactional satisfaction by calculating standardised total effects
approximated from the bias-corrected bootstrapping method (Taylor et al,
2008). Our results show that gratitude partly mediates the influence of
perceived relationship investment on purchase intent while transactional
satisfaction is a partial mediator of the influence of this construct on word
of mouth intent.

3 Discussion

This study is important to theory in several ways. First, it supports the
important role of gratitude in understanding the effects of a firm's recovery investments in complaint handling, thus extending the research
of Palmatier et al (2009) to this specific context. It notes that marketing
research that neglects gratitude and that focuses exclusively on satisfaction as a key variable may fail to capture the full effects of service
recovery. Second, the study resolves some limitations in prior research on
complaint handling in demonstrating that transactional satisfaction has

a notably stronger influence on word of mouth than purchase intent while gratitude leads to reciprocal behaviours which are focused on repurchase.

From a managerial perspective, our study takes a firm stand on the necessity of monitoring customer gratitude as a key indicator of customer service performance in the same careful manner as monitoring customer transactional satisfaction. As such, measures of gratitude must be systematically included in the satisfaction surveys that companies regularly issue. However, due to the emotion-based nature of gratitude, the resulting tendency to reciprocate may decay over time (Palmatier et al, 2009). Therefore, companies should give customers opportunities to reciprocate soon after providing them with complaint handling benefits. For example, companies could contact complainants with a coupon offer. This offer would provide the complainant an opportunity to act on his or her feelings of gratitude and most likely lead to an immediate repurchase.

Although this study expands our knowledge of complaint handling, it must be tempered with several limitations. Limitations due to the data collection procedure itself must be considered. First, our study uses a cross-sectional survey method of data collection focusing on a single interaction with customer service. Secondly, the use of a student sample is a limitation. Thirdly, the fact that the participants were asked to submit a complaint may be a limitation, even if their claims were duly motivated by dissatisfactions that actually emerged in the course of their everyday lives. Moreover, future research will need to consider additional variables. The authors recommend studying whether different types of relationship recovery investments are equally able to elicit gratitude in complaint handling. In that respect, research should consider interactional, procedural and distributive recovery investments and assess their different contributions to both gratitudinal and transactional routes to loyalty.

References

Maxham JG III, Netemeyer RG (2002) Modeling customer perceptions of complaint handling over time: the effects of perceived justice on satisfaction and intent. Journal of Retailing 78(4):239–252

Morales AC (2005) Giving firms an "E" for effort: Consumer responses to high-effort firms. Journal of Consumer Research 31(4):806–812

Orsingher C, Valentini S, Angelis M (2010) A meta-analysis of satisfaction with complaint handling in services. Journal of the Academy of Marketing Science 38(2):169–186

Palmatier RW, Jarvis CB, Bechkoff JR, Kardes FR (2009) The role of customer gratitude in relationship marketing. Journal of Marketing 73(5):1–18

Reynolds KE, Beatty SE (1999) Customer benefits and company consequences of customer-salesperson relationships in retailing. Journal of Retailing 75(1):11 – 32

Szymanski DM, Henard DH (2001) Customer satisfaction: A meta-analysis of the empirical evidence. Journal of the Academy of Marketing Science 29(1):16–35

Taylor AB, MacKinnon DP, Tein JY (2008) Tests of the three-path mediated effect. Organizational Research Methods 11(2):241–269

Tsang JA (2006) The effects of helper intention on gratitude and indebtedness. Motivation and Emotion 30:198–204

Social Access Control

Andreas C. Sonnenbichler

Abstract Facebook is one of the most important social networking sites used by over a billion of people. Facebook offers a specialized and rather limited approach to decide upon content privacy for it's users. In this paper we analyze the content protection features Facebook offers. We suggest four classes of Facebook users ranging from consumers with very limited content privacy requirements to consumers interested in fine-granular content restrictions. We want to empower the customer to choose on the access control model meeting their specific requirements. The access control model shall be customer-based and not modeled on a general Facebook-wide level. We show how such a flexible approach can be introduced into Facebook by the usage of the Access Definition and Query Language.

1 Introduction: Where Facebook Fails

In 2002, nobody knew Facebook. In 2012, Facebook got more than 1 billion users (Vance, 2012). Launched in 2004 (Phillips, 2007), Facebook today is *the* social networking platform. Probably anybody using a computer and the Internet has at least heard of Facebook. People use Facebook to post status messages, share images and videos, chat and com-

Andreas C. Sonnenbichler
Karlsruhe Institute of Technology
✉ andreas.sonnenbichler@kit.edu

CUSTOMER & SERVICE SYSTEMS
KIT SCIENTIFIC PUBLISHING
Vol. 1, No. 1, S. 133–145, 2014

DOI 10.5445/KSP/1000038784/15
ISSN 2198-8005

municate. They stay in contact with their acquaintances, share content with friends, organize parties, share travel pictures and videos, and much more. Facebook is seen to have so much influence on peoples' life, that even the term "generation Facebook" has been used (cf. Kord, 2008).

However, Facebook is not uncriticized. One of the main criticisms is that Facebook offers very limited functionality in protecting the content of users.

In this paper, we analyze the options Facebook provides to protect user data. We show that the underlying access control model is a simplified access control list (ACL). ACLs are only one way to protect data and may not be the appropriate way for every Facebook users: There may be users (e.g. companies) who require very limited content protection as every content they provide can be accessed freely. There may be security un-aware users who require only basic access control. There may be security-aware users who want to specifically decide which of their posts can be seen by whom. There even may be "paranoid" users who exactly want to define which of their content elements can be seen by which users for a specific time period. It is our target to empower Facebook customers, so that the customer can decide upon the way how his data is protected.

First, we analyze the features Facebook currently offers to protect customer content. Second, we formalize this model. Third, we discuss some options for different approaches which might be adequate for certain customer needs. Fourth, we show what is required to empower the customer to choose his preferred way of data protection.

2 Analyzing Facebook's Data Privacy Options

Which options does Facebook offer to the customer to decide upon protecting his data? When this paper was written, Facebook offered a specific way of information protection for it's users.

The menu point "menu" allows to change general account settings like the customer's name, his email address, password, and language settings. The information here is not directly related to content privacy.

The second menu point "security" offers

1. Settings allowing to change the security question a user must answer when he has forgotten his password;

Table 1 Facebook's privacy settings menu as effective on 2013-01-06 depicted as table for better readability

Privacy Settings and Tools

Who can see my stuff?	**Who can see your future posts?** You can manage the privacy of things you share by using the audience selector **right where you post**. This control remembers your selection so future posts will be shared with the same audience unless you change it.		Close
	Review all your posts and things you're tagged in		Use Activity Log
	Limit the audience for posts you've shared with friends of friends or Public?		Limit Past Posts
Who can look me up?	Who can look you up using the email address or phone number you provided?	Friends of Friends	Edit
	Do you want other search engines to link to your timeline?	Off	Edit

2. Notification settings in the case a user connects from a device he has previously not used used to connect to Facebook;

3. Settings for making mandatory use of the https protocol instead of the unencrypted http protocol.

Again, these settings provide no usage for data privacy.

The third menu option "privacy" is depicted in figure 1. The option "who can see my stuff" let the customer change the default settings who receives status updates of the customer. E.g. when this option is changed to "friends", all Facebook friends of the user receive status updates of the user. However, this option only changes the default setting. A customer may change the target group of a status update for each update specificly. This option is related to data privacy, as it allows to set a kind of protection level for a status update.

The option "review all posts and things you're tagged in" allows to review the "activity log" of the user. The "activity log" includes all status updates, content sharing and change of information in the profile of the user, e.g. if a user made new friends, posted a video, commented something, pressed the "I-like" button and so on. The offered option "review all posts and things you're tagged in" lists the activity log and let the user decide if the specific entry shall be part of his "Facebook timeline" or shall be excluded from it. The "Facebook timeline" is the set of all activities of the user ordered by their creation time. This option is related to data privacy and enables the customer to hide activities from his time-line.

The option "limit the audience for old posts on your timeline" allows a customer to restrict all content of the customer's timeline to be visible only for friends. This feature is a macro allowing to reset the protection level of old data to "friends". Actually, this is not an additional feature for data protection: The customer can manually update all old activity entries and restrict it to "friends". The feature is a comfort function allowing to modify a lot of data with only one click.

The two menu points "who can look me up" allow the customer to decide who (friends, friends of friends, public) may lookup his e-mail address and phone number. Further, the consumer can decide whether Facebook allows search engines like Google to lookup the activity data of the customer. The latter functionality only applies to content shared with "public". Thus, it is not an override to make all protected content available on a general level.

Summarizing the data protection functionality of this menu, it allows a customer to set the protection level of user activity (per default and per update), to exclude updates from the customer's timeline and to limit search functionality for the e-mail address, telephone numbers, and public content for search engines.

The menu "timeline and tagging" is depicted in figure 2. "Who can add things to my timeline" allows the customer to define which users may post content on his activity log (friends or no one) and if these posts must be reviewed by the customer before they appear in his activity log.

The menu point "review what other people see on your timeline" presents the activity log simulating being a public or a specific user. This function is very useful in verifying the security settings. However, it is not used to define security settings.

The menu points "who can see posts you've been tagged in on your timeline" and "who can see what others post on your timeline" allow a customer to limit the tagging of others users, e.g. when a friend marks the customer on an image, or posts of other users on the customer's timeline.

The menu option "review tags people add to your own posts before the tags appear on Facebook" allows the customer to decide if tags, a user assigns to his posts, e.g. comments, tags on images, have to be reviewed before they appear. The option "when you're tagged in a post, who do you want to add to the audience if they aren't already in it" has to

Table 2 Facebook's timeline and tagging menu as effective on 2013-01-06 depicted as table for better readability

Timeline and Tagging Settings

Who can add things to my timeline?	Who can post on your timeline?	Friends	Edit
	Review posts friends tag you in before they appear on your timeline?	Off	Edit
Who can see things on my timeline?	Review what other people see on your timeline		View As
	Who can see posts you've been tagged in on your timeline?	Friends	Edit
	Who can see what others post on your timeline?	Friends	Edit
How can I manage tags people add and tagging suggestions?	Review tags people add to your own posts before the tags appear on Facebook?	Off	Edit
	When you're tagged in a post, who do you want to add to the audience if they aren't already in it?	Friends	Edit
	Who sees tag suggestions when photos that look like you are uploaded? (this is not yet available to you)	Unavailable	

be explained in detail: Let a user share content. "Our" customer is then marked by somebody (e.g. the sharing user, himself or a third user), e.g. on a picture the customer is said to be someone depicted. Then, Facebook adapts the users being able to see this content depending on the menu option. It offers the settings "friends", "only me", and "customs". The latter allows to include or exclude specific users. The privacy functionality offered here is an adaption of the people being able to see content, if the customer is tagged on the content.

The last option, "who sees tag suggestions when photos that look like you are uploaded" is currently not implemented by Facebook.

Summarizing the timeline and tagging menu, it offers the following data protection functionality:

1. restrict comments and tags of other users to be reviewed by the customer,
2. define who sees tagging and posts from others in the customer's timeline,

3. define who is added to the list of users able to see content when the customer is tagged on content.

The menu "blocking" (not depicted here) allows to restrict the viewing rights of certain friends. Concerning content, when entered in the list of "restricted", these users are not perceived as friends but public users. If a user is added to this block list, Facebook handles him the same way as if he has not been defined as a friend of "our" customer.

All other menu points of Facebook's security menu (not depicted here) are not related to content privacy settings.

3 Formalizing Facebook's Security Model

In the last section we analyzed the security options Facebook offers concerning data privacy. In this section we want to formalize the access control model used by Facebook.

The access control model used by Facebook can be described by a simplified access control list (ACL). Access control lists allow to assign each object a list of users combined with their access right.

ACLs belong to discretionary access control models and are based on the famous HRU-model (Harrison et al, 1976; Harrison and Ruzzo, 1978). For background information for this kind of model type we refer to Lampson (1971, 1974), Graham and Denning (1972), and Benantar (2006).

Basically, in an ACL for each privacy protected object a list of subjects exists. Each subject is associated with a set of access rights. Objects in access control are entities to be protected (e.g. files, posts, activity list entries) and subjects are entities accessing those objects (e.g. Facebook users).

Facebook's access control model simplifies this approach in two ways: (1) It omits a general model of access rights. Only the access right "read" or "view" is modeled. (2) It assigns subject classes to users. These classes are "public", "friends of friends", "friends" and "myself". Each subject is assigned to such a class. In contrast to many other access control models, these subject classes are consumer-centered. The class "friends" differs for each subject, e.g. the class "friends" of consumer A is different from the class "friends" of user B.

An object modeled in Facebook's access control model is an activity list entry, e.g. a status update, an image, a video, a comment, and so on. A subject is a user identified by her e-mail address.

4 Empowering Facebook Customers By Choosing Customer-Based Access Control Models

We said, that we want to let the customer decide how his data is protected. Let us first define, what we exactly mean: We define a customer as a Facebook user. Technically, a customer is represented by an account identified by an unique e-mail address. We refer to a customer in the context of access control as "subject". The data of the customer consists of all content and information the customer provides, thus each activity log entry. This includes e.g. status messages ("posts"), images, videos, "I-likes", and comments on content of other people. Further more, "data" includes all profile information, e.g. his name, address, phone number, geo-location, e-mail address and so on. Also included are the friends of a user, his groups, calendar, and his "Facebook applications". To each such data entity we refer as "object".

Let us briefly suggest four Facebook user classes with different security requirements for their content:

1. There may be subjects representing companies who require limited content protection: The content they provide can be accessed freely (public access, even for non-Facebook users) or publicly to all Facebook users.
2. There may be privacy-unaware users who require only basic access control. Their content can be shared by everyone or with their friends only.
3. There may be privacy-aware users who want to specifically decide which of their content can be seen by whom. The content protection is based on a groups, thus content can be offered to close-friends, friends, acquaintances, or publicly.
4. There may be "paranoid" users who exactly want to define which of their content elements can be seen by which users for a specific time period. Paranoid consumers may want to make this decision not on a group level ("this picture may be seen by my friends") but on a very

detailed level ("this picture may be seen only by users A and B for the next two weeks").

We want to empower the customer to choose the access control model he requires. Currently, Facebook offers only one hard-coded access control model. We want to enable Facebook to offer unlimited access control models which can be defined by their customers:

One choice can be the simplified ACL model which Facebook currently uses. This is an adequate choice for the privacy-unaware user.

Another choice can be a "Bell-LaPadula"-like access control model (cf. Bell and LaPadula, 1973, 1975): Each subject is assigned a security level, e.g. "close friends", "friends", "acquaintances", "public". Each object is assigned a protection level, e.g. "close friends", "friends", "acquaintances", "public". Both lists represent a hierarchy. A subject may see content, if the subject's security level is at least as high as the object's protection level. Such a model is appropriate for a security-aware consumer as it allows him to classify his content.

A third option for the access control model chosen by the customer is a binary model: Subjects are grouped into "friends" and "public". The group assignment is done automatically by making a user a Facebook friend (or not). Each object is then assigned a flag "friend" allowing only Facebook friends to view the item or "public" making it available for anyone (even non-Facebook users). Such a model can be appropriate for a company offering most of it's content freely.

We can think of several more access control model options, e.g. a power-user model, where the model is specifically designed by and for a specific customer (for our "paranoid" user class). We do not want to deepen the possible models here, but continue with the steps required to provide a free choice for the access control model for every customer.

5 What A Customer-Based Access Control Model Requires

To empower the customer to choose his preferred access control model, the following steps have to be undertaken:

First, the access control component must be modularized. The access checks performed by Facebook's application must not assume a specific access control model and realize this through hard-coded security components. Instead, it has to be externalized to a separate software component. This requirement is basically a system-design feature which must be simply realized by Facebook's software designers. Instead of hard-coding the access control model, each request is delegated to an external component.

Second, this external access control component must be based on a meta-model for access control. This allows the component to be defined to work in a specific manner. This "specific manner" is defined by the access control model used by a specific user. This second requirement can for example be realized by the Access Definition and Query Language (ADQL) (Sonnenbichler and Geyer-Schulz, 2012; Sonnenbichler, 2013). ADQL is a software service allowing to define access control models, policies, facts and queries for access requests. The definition of the used access control model is written in a formal language, ADQL. It allows to model all previously mentioned access control models user-specifically and realize user-specific groups. Further more, existing access policies and facts can be modeled, and of course, queries can be issued and are answered if access is granted based on the current model of the user, facts, and policies.

As a short demonstration of the usage of ADQL we provide the definition of the current access control model of Facebook in ADQL:

```
# Define users, activity log entries and ACL entries
CREATE CONTAINERS users, act;
CREATE CONTAINERS acls: {public, fof, friends, hidden};

# Define content owners, friends, and activity ACLs assignments
CREATE RELATIONS owners (act, users);
CREATE RELATIONS friends (users, users);
CREATE RELATIONS acl (act, acls);

# Define policies
# The owner may always see all her content
CREATE POLICY p_owner: { (owners([act],.),[users]) };
# Public content is freely accessible
CREATE POLICY p_public: { (acl([act],.),{public}) };
# Content for friends accessible for friends
CREATE POLICY p_friends: { (acl([act],.),{friends}), (owners([act],.),
    friends([users],.)) };
# Content for friends-of-friends accessible for friends-of-friends
CREATE POLICY p_fof: { (acl([act],.),{fof}), (owners([act],.),friends(
    friends([users],.),.)) };
```

For a comprehensive description of the syntax and semantics of ADQL as well as examples of additional access control models we refer the reader to (Sonnenbichler and Geyer-Schulz, 2012; Sonnenbichler, 2013).

In the following we provide short explanations for each line of the above code:

- Line 2 defines containers which are collectors for similar entities, here for users and activities.
- Line 3 defines a container for access control lists "acls" and assigns to it entities for public, friend-of-a-friend (fof), direct friends, and hidden.
- The idea is, that an activity "act" can be linked to to an entry of the access control list. This relationship is named "acl" (please note the missing trailing 's'), linking activities from "act" to an access control list classifier from "acls" (line 8).
- Consequently, line 6 defines a relation named "owners" between activities and users,
- line 7 defines a relation named "friends" between users and users.
- Lines 1-8 define the access control model, the lines 10-18 define some example access policies:
- Line 12 creates a policy named "p_owner" allowing an owner of an activity access to the activity. The expression utilizies so-called ADQL one-filtered projections, which we do not introduce here.
- Line 14 allows access for any user to all content classified as public.
- Line 16 defined a policy granting access to all direct friends of the activity owner in the case the activity has been classified in the acl category "friends".
- Line 18 grants access to all friends-of-friends including direct friends of the activity owner, if the activity has been classified "fof".

Third, some choices for access control models shall be defined and offered for the users. A simple model shall be chosen as default. This allows in-experienced users to make use of fail-safe defaults while allowing experienced users to use exactly the model appropriate for their requirements. The third requirement should be undertaken by analyzing access control requirements of different Facebook user classes, e.g. as suggested here, companies, privacy-unaware users, privacy-aware users, and paranoid users. Specialized models for these user groups can be defined and offered.

6 Conclusion

Facebook offers basic functionality to let a customer protect his data, e.g. status updates, videos, images, comments and so on. We analyzed the access control model offered by Facebook. We came to the result, that this access control model can be implemented by a simplified access control list (ACL) model: Access rights are omitted and represented only by "read" or "view". Subjects (users) are assigned to the user-specific subject classes "public", "friends of friends", "friends" and "myself".

Security requirements of Facebook may differ a lot based on the type of user. We suggested four user classes:

1. Companies with limited access control requirements offering their content for public access or Facebook "friends".
2. Privacy-unaware consumers who are interested in a simple protection allowing them to share content with everyone or with their friends only.
3. Privacy-aware consumers who want to decide for each of their content elements who shall receive it. The decision should be made on a group level, thus content can be shared for "close friends", "friends", "acquaintances", "public".
4. Paranoid consumers who want to make this decision not on a group level ("this picture may be seen by my friends") but on a detailed level ("this picture may be seen only by users A and B for the next two weeks").

To empower the consumer to let him choose his preferred access control model, three steps have to be undertaken:

1. The access control model must be modularized and not hard-coded.
2. A software component allowing to define the user-specific access control model must be used.
3. Some choices for access control models must be designed and offered for the user.

We sketched how step 2 can be implemented by the Access Definition and Query Language (ADQL) for the current access control model of Facebook.

References

Bell DE, LaPadula LJ (1973) Secure computer systems: Mathematical foundations and model. Mitre Corporation, Bedford, MA, USA 1(M74-244):42, DOI 10.1016/0169-7552(95)00081-X

Bell DE, LaPadula LJ (1975) Secure Computer Systems: Mathematical Foundations and Model. M74-244, Mitre Corporation, Bedford, MA, USA

Benantar M (2006) Access Control Systems. Springer, New York

Graham GS, Denning PJ (1972) Protection: Principles and practice. In: Proceedings of the May 16-18, 1972, Spring Joint Computer Conference, ACM, New York, AFIPS '72 (Spring), pp 417–429, DOI 10.1145/1478873.1478928

Harrison MA, Ruzzo WL, Ullman JD (1976) Protection in operating systems. Communications of the ACM 19(8):461–471, DOI 10.1145/360303.360333

Harrison MH, Ruzzo WL (1978) Monotonic protection systems. In: Demilo R (ed) Foundations of Secure Computations, Academic Press, pp 337–365

Kord JI (2008) Understanding the Facebook Generation: A Study of the Relationship Between Online Social Networking and Academic and Social Integration and Intentions to Re-enroll. ProQuest Information and Learning Company, Ann Arbor, Michigan, USA

Lampson BW (1971) Protection. In: Proceedings of the Fifth Princeton Symposium on Information Sciences and Systems, Princeton University, pp 437–443

Lampson BW (1974) Protection (reprint). ACM SIGOPS Operating Systems Review 8:18–24, DOI 10.1145/775265.775268

Phillips S (2007) A brief history of facebook. The Guardian 2007-07-25

Sonnenbichler A (2013) An Access Definition and Query Language: Towards a Unified Access Control Model. KIT Scientific Publishing, Karlsruhe, Germany

Sonnenbichler AC, Geyer-Schulz A (2012) ADQL: A Flexible Access Definition and Query Language to Define Access Control Models. In: Samarati P (ed) Proceedings of the International Conference on Security and Cryptography 2012, The Institute for Systems and Technologies of Information, Control and Communication (INSTICC), Rome

Vance A (2012) Facebook: The making of 1 billion users. Bloomberg Businessweek 2012-10-04

Three Perspectives for Making Loyalty Programs More Effective

Lena Steinhoff and Robert W. Palmatier

Abstract Loyalty programs are an ubiquitous instrument of customer relationship management. However, many loyalty programs perform poorly, which ultimately results in their abolition. Among both marketing managers and researchers, reasons for loyalty program failure are far from clear. The aim of this research is to enhance our understanding of loyalty program effectiveness. We propose a broadened framework for analyzing loyalty program performance which relies on three perspectives: a customer portfolio perspective, a reward elements perspective, and a reward delivery perspective. Further on, we identify three psychological mechanisms, i.e. customer gratitude, customer status, and customer unfairness as the positive and negative forces mediating loyalty programs' impact on performance outcomes. We validate our framework in two experimental studies and one field study.

Lena Steinhoff
University of Paderborn, Marketing Department, Paderborn, Germany,
✉ lena.steinhoff@wiwi.upb.de

Robert W. Palmatier
University of Washington, Michael G. Foster School of Business, Seattle, WA, USA,
✉ palmatrw@uw.edu

CUSTOMER & SERVICE SYSTEMS
KIT SCIENTIFIC PUBLISHING
Vol. 1, No. 1, S. 147–152, 2014

DOI 10.5445/KSP/1000038784/16
ISSN 2198-8005

1 Introduction

Loyalty programs, both in business practice and as a focus of marketing research, have become popular over the past decade. With US companies annually spending more than $1.2 billion on their programs, program participation topping 1.8 billion households and the average US household subscribing to 14 different programs (Ferguson and Hlavinka, 2009; Wagner et al, 2009), loyalty programs without any doubt "have become a key component of customer relationship management" (Kivetz and Simonson, 2003, p. 454). However, the financial performance of loyalty programs rarely meets expectations (Dowling and Uncles, 1997; Henderson et al, 2011; Meyer-Waarden, 2012), often resulting in their abolition (Nunes and Drèze, 2006). While marketing researchers substantiate the marginal effectiveness of some loyalty programs (Meyer-Waarden, 2007; Meyer-Waarden and Benavent, 2009; Shugan, 2005), to date "it is far from clear what sets a successful [loyalty program] apart from an unsuccessful one" (Kumar and Reinartz, 2006, p. 172). In view of these mixed effects, the focus of this research is to improve our understanding of loyalty program effectiveness.

2 Perspectives for Understanding the Effectiveness of Loyalty Programs

We propose that the framework for understanding the effectiveness of loyalty programs needs to be expanded in three key ways in order to draw a more holistic picture of loyalty program performance. Fig. 1 outlines our overall framework for a typical airline loyalty program.

1. First, a *customer portfolio perspective* should be utilized when evaluating loyalty program performance to account for the effect of a loyalty program on both target and bystander customers (point 1 in Fig. 1). While the exclusive rewards rendered to target customers may positively affect their receivers, companies do not account for how their loyalty program might impact those customers around the focal customers, i.e. the bystander customers. Unintended negative reactions of bystanders might hurt the overall effectiveness of a loyalty program. Thus, we do not consider solely the target customer,

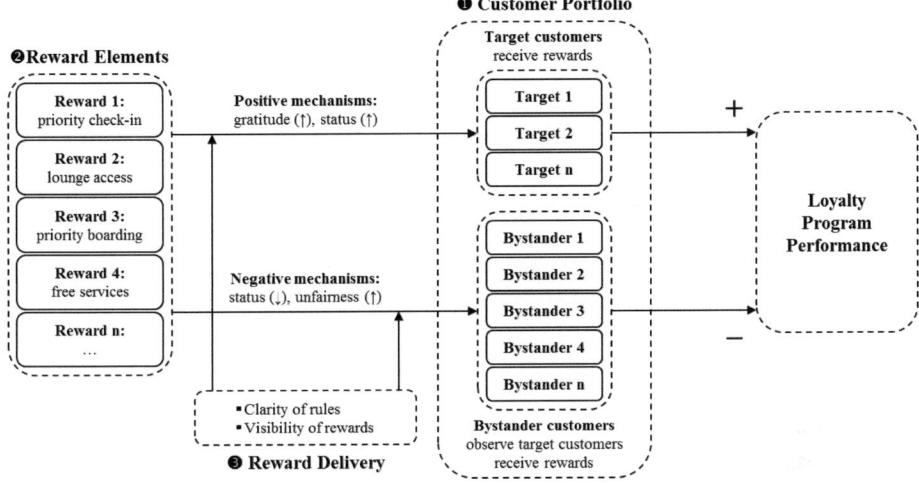

Fig. 1 Framework for understanding the effectiveness of loyalty programs

but rather the whole customer portfolio as the unit of analysis when determining loyalty program performance.

2. Second, a *reward elements perspective* should be utilized when evaluating loyalty program performance to account for the differential and potentially opposing effects of each reward element of the program (point 2 in Fig. 1). Extant research typically investigates loyalty programs on an aggregate level. However, since most loyalty programs consist of multiple rewards, both positive and negative effects of specific reward elements on both target and bystander customers may be masked. Disentangling rewards and their respective impact enables us to identify and understand the drivers and impediments of loyalty program effectiveness.

3. Third, a *reward delivery perspective* should be utilized when evaluating loyalty program performance to account for the differential and potentially opposing effects of reward delivery on the linkages between specific reward elements and target or bystander customers' responses (point 3 in Fig. 1). Loyalty program effectiveness might be contingent on the way rewards are delivered. Including reward delivery into loyalty program analyses enables managers to not only evaluate what rewards to adopt, but also how to implement them to accomplish optimal performance impact.

3 Loyalty-Influencing Mechanisms

Expanding our framework to include the effects of bystanders, multiple reward elements, and reward delivery on loyalty program performance, we suggest three psychological mechanisms to capture the link between loyalty programs and performance outcomes.

1. First, *customer gratitude* represents the emotional appreciation for benefits received involving a desire to reciprocate (Emmons and McCullough, 2004; Palmatier et al, 2009). Gratitude has been identified as an important positive mechanism linking rewards to performance.
2. Second, *customer status* is defined as the customer's perception of holding an elevated position within a firm's customer hierarchy (Drèze and Nunes, 2009; Festinger, 1954). Experiencing preferential treatment bestowed by the firm enhances target customers' perceived status. Indeed, due to its inherently relative nature, status acts as doubleedged sword: Making target customers feel superior status naturally leads to perceptions of inferior status among bystander customers.
3. Third, *customer unfairness* denotes the customers' view of the degree to which the ratio of their received outcomes relative to their inputs as compared to the corresponding input-outcome ratios of other customers is inequitable (Adams, 1965; Samaha et al, 2011). Unfairness issues are likely to arise among bystanders and can trigger severe negative reactions.

4 Conclusion

We empirically test our framework in three complementary studies. In Studies 1 and 2, we use an experimental approach in an airline and hotel context. In Study 3, we assess our conceptual model in a field setting for actual airline loyalty programs. Results support the validity of our broadened approach in analyzing loyalty program effectiveness. Our contributions can be summarized as follows.

1. First, we demonstrate that in order to get a complete picture of loyalty program performance, we need to consider the whole customer

portfolio affected by a loyalty program. We simultaneously account for target as well as bystander customer effects when analyzing loyalty program effectiveness.

2. Second, we disentangle the differential effects of specific loyalty program rewards on target and bystander customers. Analyzing customer responses towards typical rewards employed by airlines in their loyalty programs, we underscore the importance of a detailed assessment of each reward in order to make informed decisions on the introduction, adaptation or abolition of rewards.

3. Third, we delineate how the delivery of rewards varies their impact on loyalty program performance. By showing that the effects of loyalty programs on both target and bystander customers are either emphasized or diminished depending on reward delivery, we highlight the importance of companies' design decisions.

4. Fourth, we establish a "battery" of positive and negative forces linking loyalty programs to performance outcomes. Whereas gratitude and superior status build target customer loyalty, inferior status and unfairness destroy bystander customer loyalty. When assessing their loyalty programs, managers should take these psychological mechanisms into account.

References

Adams JS (1965) Inequity in social exchange. In: Berkowitz L (ed) Advances in Experimental Social Psychology, vol 2, Academic Press, pp 267–299

Dowling GR, Uncles M (1997) Do customer loyalty programs really work? Sloan Management Review 38(4):71–82

Drèze X, Nunes JC (2009) Feeling superior: The impact of loyalty program structure on consumers' perceptions of status. Journal of Consumer Research 35(6):890–905

Emmons RA, McCullough ME (2004) The Psychology of Gratitude. Series in Affective Science, Oxford University Press, USA

Ferguson R, Hlavinka K (2009) The Big Sort: The 2009 COLLOQUY Loyalty Marketing Census. Loyalty One/COLLOQUY, Cincinnati

Festinger L (1954) A theory of social comparison processes. Human Rela-
    tions 7(2):117–140

Henderson CM, Beck JT, Palmatier RW (2011) Review of the theoretical
    underpinnings of loyalty programs. Journal of Consumer Psychology
    21(3):256–276

Kivetz R, Simonson I (2003) The idiosyncratic fit heuristic: Effort advan-
    tage as a determinant of consumer response to loyalty programs. Jour-
    nal of Marketing Research 40:454–467

Kumar V, Reinartz WJ (2006) Customer relationship management: A
    database approach. Wiley, New York

Meyer-Waarden L (2007) The effects of loyalty programs on customer life-
    time duration and share of wallet. Journal of Retailing 83(2):223–236

Meyer-Waarden L (2012) Management de la fidélisation: Développer la
    relation client : de la stratégie aux technologies numériques. Vuibert,
    Paris

Meyer-Waarden L, Benavent C (2009) Grocery retail loyalty program
    effects: Self-selection or purchase behavior change? Journal of the
    Academy of Marketing Science 37(3):345–358

Nunes JC, Drèze X (2006) Your loyalty program is betraying you. Harvard
    Business Review 84(4):124–131

Palmatier RW, Jarvis CB, Bechkoff JR, Kardes FR (2009) The role of
    customer gratitude in relationship marketing. Journal of Marketing
    73(5):1–18

Samaha SA, Palmatier RW, Dant RP (2011) Poisoning relationships: Per-
    ceived unfairness in channels of distribution. Journal of Marketing
    75(3):99–117

Shugan SM (2005) Brand loyalty programs: Are they shams? Marketing
    Science 24(2):185–193

Wagner T, Hennig-Thurau T, Rudolph T (2009) Does customer demotion
    jeopardize loyalty? Journal of marketing 73(3):69–85

Lead-Users vs. Emergent Nature Consumers for Marketing Co-Creation: Are They Really Different?

Eric Vernette and Linda Hamdi-Kidar

Abstract This research extends Hoffman et al (2010)'s work on the relationship between two key targets for co-creation: Emergent-Nature Consumers (ENC) and Lead-Users (LU). These authors have shown that an ENC - who can innovate in any domain, could be more effective than a LU- who innovates in one specific-domain, for the development of new product concepts. We show that these two innovating users have common conceptual roots and that ENC character trait corresponds to an extension of LU characteristics to all product domains. We also show that the ENC trait is an antecedent of specific-domain lead-usership. It finally appears that ENC and LU characteristics are crucial determinants for engagement in co-creation activities.

1 Introduction

Marketing co-creation is a topic of high relevance for both academia and business practice. Business managers and marketers increasingly try to identify and to assess possibilities to integrate cutting-edge or tech savvy

Eric Vernette
Center for Research in Management, Université Toulouse I Capitole, UMR CNRS 5303
✉ eric.vernette@ut-capitole.fr

Linda Hamdi-Kidar
Center for Research in Management, Université Toulouse I Capitole, UMR CNRS 5303
✉ linda.hamdi@iae-toulouse.fr

CUSTOMER & SERVICE SYSTEMS
KIT SCIENTIFIC PUBLISHING
Vol. 1, No. 1, S. 153–163, 2014

DOI 10.5445/KSP/1000038784/17
ISSN 2198-8005

customers in their innovation process to avoid future risks of market failure (Von Hippel, 2011). Furthermore, from an academic perspective, the increasing interest in the field of co-creation has received considerable attention in the venue of Vargo and Lusch (2008)'s Service-Dominant Logic.

Marketing literature suggests exploiting the innovating potential of two types of consumers: Lead-Users (LU) and Emergent-Nature Consumers (ENC). The advantages of the first are widely recognized: They are ahead of the market trends and expect high benefits from a solution to their advanced needs in one specific domain (Von Hippel, 1986). The assets of ENCs for marketing have been highlighted more recently by Hoffman et al (2010): "these consumers are really helpful in developing product concepts, particularly in the consumer goods industry; moreover, they seem able to develop any product concepts that mainstream consumers found significantly more appealing and useful than concepts developed by lead-users". This result leads to focus on ENCs to the detriment of LUs despite the recommendations of much previous research (e.g. Franke et al, 2006; Lilien et al, 2002). The Emergent nature construct is conceptualized as a character trait applicable to all product or service categories.

If we want to shed light on this issue, we need to re-examine and compare the conceptual foundations of these two constructs. The choice of the right target for a marketing co-creation strategy remains a tricky one: Should it aim at the specialists of a single product category (i.e. LUs), or should it rather aim at more general consumers (i.e. ENCs)? What are their respective competences and willingness to get engaged?

Hence, this article aims to assess the degree of convergence and discrimination between these two concepts to increase our knowledge of the relationship between them at both theoretical and managerial levels.

2 Co-creating with innovative consumers

2.1 Lead-user: product focused vs. general trait

Lead-usership is generally appraised for a given product/service market. However, according to (Churchill et al, 2009, p. 9), identifying LUs in one product category leads to the inclusion of several different markets:

1. LUs in the target application and market,
2. LUs in similar applications in advanced analog markets and those
3. with respect to important attributes of problems faced by users in the target market.

In the same vein, Von Hippel et al (2011) propose an overall understanding of the LU when they study the innovations developed by users in the household sector. In their research, the LU is no longer studied within a specific product or service, but is aggregated on a set of connected markets related to the household sector. For their part, Jeppesen and Laursen (2009) took this further, proposing a global LU concept: They completely disregard the product category and measure the individual perception of lead-usership with regard to the whole products/services range. Extending these findings to our research, we could assume a global LU who transcends product or service category. This global LU would be a consumer, who is dissatisfied by a great number of products and services available on markets, but unlike other discontented individuals, the global LU [1] regularly invents or experiments with all sorts of original solutions to solve the various problems encountered; these solutions anticipate future trends in these markets.

2.2 Emergent-nature consumers vs. lead-users

Hoffman et al (2010) define the Emergent nature consumers as individuals who have a "unique capability to imagine or envision how concepts might be further developed so that they will be successful in the main-

---

[1] We use the term "global LU" (i.e. lead-user in any product/service category) in opposition to the traditional LU construct (i.e. lead-user in one product/service category or domain-specific) that we interchangeably call "specialized LU" or "specific LU".

stream marketplace". Their ideas are innovative and capable of resolving all kinds of problems while also anticipating future market trends.

In comparison, specialized LUs' ideas are original but they anticipate needs for a single market. By extension, ideas of "global LUs" are also probably original but anticipate needs for any market. This large spectrum requires a particular aptitude for original ideas and for feeling emerging needs before others do; this aptitude reflects personality traits like originality, imagination, creativity and anticipation that are shared by ENCs.

According to Hoffman et al (2010), the major difference between ENCs and specialized LUs (i.e. traditional LU construct) is the expertise, arguing that the first "not have to be experts in the product category". However, Von Hippel (2011) takes the opposite position when he specifies that the value of the products created by LUs is not in their product engineering. ENCs and specialized LUs share several common traits: They are innovators in the given product or service category, but they are not necessarily experts in that category. In addition, open-mindedness, creativity and rationality (characteristics of ENCs), create a favorable context for lead-usership in any product category. Henceforth, if ENC is a character trait, it is coherent to think that it is an antecedent of the specific LU characteristics: Having this trait would thus increase the probability of being a LU in a given product category. If this was not the case, it would be difficult to explain the fairly high correlations (0.39 and 0.48) obtained by Hoffman et al (2010), between the ENC trait and the fact of being a LU in a very specific product category (i.e. consumer home delivery goods).

2.3 Emergent-nature consumers, lead-users and engagement in co-creation

ENCs are attractive for co-creation because they "imagine or envision how concepts might be further developed so that they will be successful in the mainstream marketplace". In the same way, LUs are natural and efficient targets for co-creation (Thomke and Von Hippel, 2002): "The best prospects are customers that have a strong need for developing custom products quickly and frequently". For example, 3M estimates internally that ideas from groups of LUs are worth $146 million, equivalent to 8 times the sum expected from the forecast sales resulting from traditional working groups (Lilien et al, 2002). Other studies show that LUs are more efficient for co-creation than ordinary consumers (e.g. Jeppesen and Laursen, 2009; Magnusson, 2009).

Contrary to what might be supposed, it is not necessarily brand fans who are the most inclined to co-create; identification with the brand is not related to participation in innovative activities (Füller et al, 2008). We might expect that LUs would engage in co-creation collaborative platforms (e.g. Thomke and Von Hippel, 2002), especially since they make great use of online and offline community resources (Bilgram et al, 2008; Franke et al, 2006).

3 Research Methods

In this research, we assess individuals' specific lead-usership in the field of video games. We collected data through a web-based questionnaire survey. We collected 995 completed questionnaires administered in September 2011 on a representative sample of the French population over 16 years of age. The sample was selected according to the quota method (age, region, sex and level of education)[2]. A filter question eliminated consumers who rarely or never play video games; this amounted to 45.8% of the original population. Our final sample comprised 456 individuals.

The measures are all one-dimensional, five-point Likert scales. English scales were translated and adapted to French through back-translation. Specific lead-usership was measured with a four-item scale adapted to video games from Béji-Bécheur and Goletty (2007) ($\alpha = .856$). To assess global lead-usership (Appendix 1), we adapted the same scale by simple transposition to a context of overall consumption of products/services: We replaced each item of the scale referring to video game with products and services, following the same procedure as Jeppesen and Laursen (2009) ($\alpha = .817$). To measure emergent nature, the eight-item scale developed and validated by Hoffman et al (2010) was used ($\alpha = .836$). Consumer engagement in co-creation is seen as "co-production of contents between

---

[2] The sample was taken from an open-access panel managed by a European market research company.

Table 1 Convergent and discriminant validity of the different measures of the concepts

	Emergent-nature	Global LU	Specific LU
Average Variance Explained	0.65	0.53	0.62
	Squared Correlations		
Emergent-nature			
Global LU	0.95		
Specific LU	0.27	0.41	

company and customers" (Gambetti and Graffigna, 2010). It is measured with four items ($\alpha = .810$).

4 Results

First, we assess the convergent and discriminant validity of the measures with the Fornell and Larcker (1981)'s criteria[3] (Table 1). All the AVE coefficients are above 0.50, so that the convergent validity among these three measures is established. On the one hand, we observe that the measure of ENC trait shows discriminant validity with the measure of specific LU in video games ($r^2 = 0.27 < 0.65$ and 0.62). We obtain a similar result when comparing between specific LU in video games and "global LU" ($r^2 = 0.41 < 0.53$ and 0.62). On the other hand, our measure of "global LU" does not allow us to discriminate this concept from that of ENC ($r^2 = 0.95 > 0.53$ and 0.65): the two constructs are highly correlated.

Consequently, the constructs ENC and global LU relate to the same concept. Symmetrically, our results also show that the ENC is conceptually different from the specific LU, thus confirming the results reported by Hoffman et al (2010).

Based on our previous analysis of concepts, we assume that the ENC (or global LU) is an antecedent to the specific LU. In other words, the more an individual possesses the ENC (or global LU) traits, the more he/she will tend to be a specific LU in a given product category. We constructed two series of structural models on this basis; the first retains ENC as a predictor of specific LU and the second global LU (Fig. 1).

---

[3] The measures must have an AVE (average variance explained) above 0.50 and share more variance with their indicators (AVE) than with the measures of other concepts.

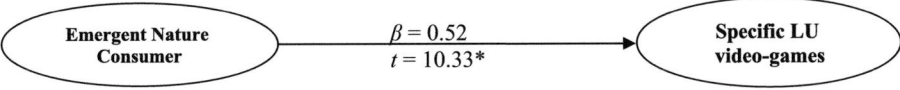

SMC = 0.27; Fit statistics: $\chi 2$/df = 2.53 (134.3/53); GFI = 0.95; IFI = 0.97; CFI = 0.97.

SMC = 0.41; Fit statistics: $\chi 2$/df = 3.62 (68.79/19); GFI = 0.96; IFI = 0.97; CFI = 0.97.
* $p < 0.001$

Fig. 1 Relations between the ENC (global LU) and the specific LU in video games

Table 2 The relationships of ENC, global LU and specific LU with marketing co-creation

	Structural Models Predictor variable	Dependent variables Engagement in co-creation
Emergent-Nature Consumer	Structural Coefficients	$\beta = 0.50$; $t = 9.23$* SMC = 0.25
	Fit statistics	$\chi 2/df = 1.63$ (86.52/53); GFI = 0.96; IFI = 0.99; CFI = 0.99
Global LU	Structural Coefficients	$\beta = 0.57$; $t = 8.97$* SMC = 0.32
	Fit indices	$\chi 2/df = 1.93$ (36.79/19); GFI = 0.98; IFI = 0.98; CFI = 0.98
Specific LU (video-games)	Structural Coefficients	$\beta = 0.51$; t = 8.91*SMC = 0.26
	Fit indices	$\chi 2/df = 1.78$ (33.89/19); GFI = 0.98; IFI = 0.99; CFI = 0.99

* $p < 0.001$

Figure 1 shows that the structural coefficients are both significant: the ENC and the global LU characteristics are two antecedents to the specific LU in a given product category – here, video games. We also observe that the beta between global LU or ENC and specific LU are high and comparable: this result confirms the similarity between the two concepts (ie. global LU and ENC).

We created a series of structural models based on single relationships between one of the three predictor variables (ENC, global LU and specific LU) and the dependent variable - engagement in co-creation.

Table 2 shows that the more an individual has an ENC (or global LU or specific LU) character, the readier he/she will be to get engaged in marketing co-creation whatever the product category.

5 Discussion and Implications

From a theoretical perspective, an important result is that a great number of the essential characteristics of ENC merge with those of "global LU". These two constructs translate similar traits: When confronted with a given material problem, such individuals do not remain passive. They have a predisposition to be a lead-user in any product or service category. An interesting analogy could be made with the debate between opinion leaders and market mavens. The latter may have broader expertise over several product categories even if overlaps are limited: only 13% are opinion leaders in four or more product categories (King and Summers, 1970). In counterpart, market maven is characterized by general marketplace expertise, and correlates with opinion leadership($r = 0.22$) (Feick and Price, 1987). Similarly, we show that ENC and global LU are both characterized by a general ideation expertise, but specific LU has a more product focused expertise. The correlation between the global and specific LU is moderate ($r = 0.27$).

We can certainly observe that at the time of writing, few if any academic articles dealing with the concept of ENC have been published since that of Hoffman et al (2010), whereas the literature on specific LU's has been prolific. We nevertheless think that the ENC remains of interest for two reasons. Firstly, the ENC poses the question of identifying specific traits in consumers that find it easy to imagine original products. Finally, according to Hoffman et al (2010), ENCs develop more attractive concepts than specific LUs do. This result seems somewhat counter-intuitive. Replications are thus necessary: It would be interesting to repeat the experiment on other products and services, not only for the ideation phase, but also for the prototype development phases. Such replications would allow us to answer another important underlying question: Should marketing co-creation try to seek out individuals with particular personality traits (e.g. creativity, rational thinking, etc.), that is, ENC or global LU, or should it rather seek individuals who know more about the relevant

Appendix 1: Items for measuring Specific-domain Lead-usership - video games

1. I had expectations on the use of "video games" long before others
2. I have had ideas on how to improve the use of "video games" that have since been taken up by others
3. Today, "video games" on the market eventually meet needs that I have had for a long time
4. My ideas about "video games" are innovative compared to current practices

product category (specific LU)? In other words, is a contingent approach (individual competences in a particular product category) to marketing co-creation more, equally or less efficient than a trait-based approach?

From a managerial perspective, our results reinforce the interest of focusing on LUs or ENCs for co-creation, rather than aiming at ordinary consumers. Indeed, the more an individual is ENC, global LU or specific LU, the more he/she is willing to engage in co-creation activities.

Our results confirm the existence of a solid correlation between the ENC traits and the specialized LU characteristics and show that the first are an antecedent of the second. These two points are of interest for research institutes and marketing managers since according to a recent research, co-production was found to be negatively related to willingness to pay (Bilstein et al, 2012; Hogreve, 2013). Thus, it could be relevant to constitute a wide consumer panel with ENCs (or global LUs). Such a panel can be built at a lower cost, for these consumers are more inclined to participate in panels than ordinary consumers: As we have shown, they are prepared to get engaged in marketing co-creation. In a second phase, if necessary, it is easy to filter this panel according to the category of product or service in order to select only specialized LUs who are competent for co-creation in the required domain.

References

Béji-Bécheur A, Goletty M (2007) Lead user et leader d'opinion: Deux cibles majeures au service de l'innovation. Décisions Marketing 48(4):21–34

Bilgram V, Brem A, Voigt KI (2008) User-centric innovations in new product development - systematic identification of lead users harnessing interactive and collaborative online-tools. International Journal of Innovation Management 12(3):419–458

Bilstein N, Fahr R, Hogreve J, Sichtmann C (2012) Paying for a higher workload? an experimental investigation of the relationship between customer's co-production and willingness-to-pay. In: Proceedings of the 41st European Marketing Academy Conference (EMAC), Lisbon, Portugal

Churchill J, Von Hippel E, Sonnack M (2009) Lead-user Project Handbook: A practical guide for lead-user teams. MIT Press, Cambridge, Mass

Feick LF, Price LL (1987) The market maven: A diffuser of marketplace information. Journal of Marketing 51(1):83–97

Fornell C, Larcker DF (1981) Evaluating structural equation models with unobservable variables and measurement error. Journal of Marketing Research 18(1):39–50

Franke N, Von Hippel E, Schreier M (2006) Finding commercially attractive user innovations: A test of lead-user theory. Journal of Product Innovation Management 23(4):301–315

Füller J, Matzler K, Hoppe M (2008) Brand community members as a source of innovation. Journal of Product Innovation Management 25(6):608–619

Gambetti RC, Graffigna G (2010) The concept of engagement: A systematic analysis of the ongoing marketing debate. International Journal of Market Research 52(6):801–826

Hoffman DL, Kopalle PK, Novak TP (2010) The "right" consumers for better concepts: Identifying consumers high in emergent nature to develop new product concepts. Journal of Marketing Research 47(5):854–865

Hogreve J (2013) I don't work for free! the influence of customer's co-production on willingness to pay. In: Proceedings of the Customer Empowerment Workshop

Jeppesen LB, Laursen K (2009) The role of lead users in knowledge sharing. Research Policy 38(10):1582–1589

King CW, Summers JO (1970) Overlap of opinion leadership across consumer product categories. Journal of Marketing Research 7(1):43–50

Lilien GL, Morrison PD, Searls K, Sonnack M, Von Hippel E (2002) Performance assessment of the lead user idea-generation process for new product development. Management Science 48(8):1042–1059

Magnusson P (2009) Exploring the contributions of involving ordinary users in ideation of technology-based services. Journal of product innovation management 26(5):578–593

Thomke S, Von Hippel E (2002) Customers as innovators: A new way to create value. Harvard Business Review 80(4):74–81

Vargo SL, Lusch RF (2008) Service-dominant logic: continuing the evolution. Journal of the Academy of Marketing Science 36(1):1–10, DOI 10.1007/s11747-007-0069-6

Von Hippel E (1986) Lead users: A source of novel product concepts. Management Science 32(7):791–805

Von Hippel E (2011) The user innovation revolution. MIT Sloan Management Review September 1–7

Von Hippel E, Ogawa S, De Jong JPJ (2011) The age of the consumer-innovator. MIT Sloan Management Review 53(1):27–35

Index